D0207627

THE CLOSE-KNIT CIRCLE

**Recent Titles in
the American Subcultures**

Vegetarians and Vegans in America Today
Karen Iacobbo and Michael Iacobbo

THE CLOSE-KNIT CIRCLE

American Knitters Today

Kerry Wills

AMERICAN SUBCULTURES
Bruce Jackson, Series Editor

Westport, Connecticut
London

Library of Congress Cataloging-in-Publication Data

Wills, Kerry, 1968–
   The close-knit circle : American knitters today / Kerry Wills.
      p. cm. — (American subcultures, ISSN 1559–2375)
   Includes bibliographical references and index.
   ISBN-13: 978–0–275–99246–0 (alk. paper)
   ISBN-10: 0–275–99246–2 (alk. paper)
  1. Knitting—Social aspects—United States. I. Title.
II. Title: American knitters today.
  TT819.U6W55 2007
   746.43'2041—dc22   2007000071

British Library Cataloguing in Publication Data is available.

Library of Congress Catalog Card Number: 2007000071
ISBN-13: 978–0–275–99246–0
ISBN-10: 0–275–99246–2
ISSN: 1559–2375

First published in 2007

Praeger Publishers, 88 Post Road West, Westport, CT 06881
An imprint of Greenwood Publishing Group, Inc.
www.praeger.com

Printed in the United States of America

The paper used in this book complies with the
Permanent Paper Standard issued by the National
Information Standards Organization (Z39.48–1984).

10 9 8 7 6 5 4 3 2 1

Copyright Acknowledgments

Every reasonable effort has been made to trace the owners of copyright materials in this book, but in some instances this has proven impossible. The author and publisher will be glad to receive information leading to more complete acknowledgments in subsequent printings of the book and in the meantime extend their apologies for any omissions.

To Meredith, who endured my tears, curses, and hours of befuddlement when she taught me to knit. She gave me a lifelong delight and obsession.

CONTENTS

SERIES FOREWORD

The guiding spirit for American Subcultures is not an anthropologist or sociologist or social scientist or a theorist of any kind. Rather, it is the greatest American poet of them all, Walt Whitman, proclaiming in "Song of Myself":

> Do I contradict myself?
> Very well then I contradict myself,
> (I am large, I contain multitudes.)

As do we all. No one belongs to and is fully identified or explained by membership in only one subculture, though at a particular moment in time one subculture may be dominant in any of us.

When we're traveling abroad, we may think of ourselves (and be identified by others) as Americans, but most of the time that category is too gross to be of any use for anything but caricature. It covers too many things that are not us, and it omits too many things that are. We are, in the course of our days, people who live in this town or that city, people who are gay or straight, people who work at this trade or that profession. We are bowlers, machinists, dancers, lawyers, ball players, students, teachers, cooks, eaters, lovers, bikers, cross-dressers, knitters, Vietnam vets, Gulf war (I) vets, Gulf war (II) vets, cops, crooks, body-builders, surfers, novelists, nudists, Buddhists, Muslims, Jews, Christians, born-agains, drug addicts, Internet addicts, street people . . .

A subculture is part of a larger culture. In ordinary scholarly or popular discourse, the meaning of *subculture* depends on who is talking and what he or she is talking about. If the subject is North America, a subculture could be anything from local Little League team players and their parents to lawyers or Jews or Yankees or Westerners. But even those categories are often too broad to be of use. If the subject is Westerners, then further subcultures are coastal, mountain, high plains, water-rich, water-poor, farming, ranching Westerners. You can slice the apple a hundred ways, nearly all of them valid.

An African American musician from New York who went to Harvard and who is on active duty in the reserves in Iraq is at once a member of several distinct subcultures. Army reservists in Iraq are most obviously members of the subculture of the American military, but they are also members of such more specific military subcultures as Special Forces or the medical corps or helicopter pilots or the infantry. They are also as much members of the subcultures of Tennessee farmers or Los Angeles bus drivers or New York schoolteachers as they were when they left home. A man serving a prison sentence is most obviously and immediately a member of the subculture of convicts, but he is also a white or black or Hispanic or Native American or Asian. Neither the reservists nor the convicts leave those other parts of their experience and knowledge at home with their civilian clothes.

An interest or a behavior is not enough to define a subculture. Everyone eats and most people run sometimes, but eaters don't constitute a subculture on the basis of that fact alone and neither do people who run only to catch the bus. But vegetarians who are part of the community of information of other vegetarians are members of a subculture, as are runners who take part in serious running events. Likewise oenophiles and professional cooks and artisan bakers.

Which is to say, every one of us is not only a resident of this or that geographical place but we are also a member of this or that community of interest, concern, ethnicity, behavior: our lives are in our subcultures, several of them, simultaneously or alternatively.

And that is what the books in American Subcultures, each of them written by experts in that particular field or area, are about. Each explores a specific piece of the great range of interest and behavior that in sum comprise the essence of American life.

In *The Close-Knit Circle: American Knitters Today*, Kerry Wills explores the history and huge range of behaviors and communities that make up the subculture of American knitters. It is a subculture that has roots in the distant past, one that has equal room for artists and hobbyists, for people who work alone and for people who work in company; it is a subculture that brings together people who might otherwise never have occasion to talk, share, and hang out. It is a world of endless possibility defined by an activity that serves countless needs and ends. Kerry Wills introduces us to a subculture that does all of the useful and interesting things subcultures do, and she writes about those things with wit, verve, insight, and energy.

Bruce Jackson
Series Editor

PREFACE

One of the most remarkable aspects of the American subculture of young and new knitters is that it is so welcoming to newcomers. It's as if this group's members all know they have a secret too amazing to keep to themselves. As I researched this book, I rarely encountered resistance from anyone when I sought an interview, a fact, or a photograph. More often, I was shocked by the willingness of busy people to drop everything and help me out. After a decade as a daily news reporter, during which I wrestled daily with reluctant sources, I was delighted to find my intrusions into knitters' lives greeted with friendliness and enthusiasm. Over and over, I spoke with notable knitters for the first time and sensed I was speaking with old friends. The effusive and generous spirit of this subculture is among the main reasons I felt compelled to write about it, and I hope that you, the reader, will feel the same warm embrace as you turn the following pages.

I must thank many people for their time, information, and willingness to let me into their close-knit world. Elinore Kaufman and Maria Alvarez are two young women whose knitting circle I first invaded early in 2005. Knowing I was the wife of a future Lutheran pastor, they were good enough to trust me and welcome me into their specialized club, Knitters for Choice. Their warmth and acceptance gave me much courage, and, as a first-time author, I truly needed that kind of support.

From then on, I was able to get to know so many talented, fascinating, and very busy people. Many of these knitters have worked knitting into a career, and so speaking to me was a notable act of trust. I want to thank them explicitly here. To Debbie Stoller, who has reclaimed knitting for feminists everywhere and whose books have revived this long-neglected craft, I owe great thanks. Debbie walks the talk. She had never met or heard of me, and yet she called me direct at home in response to my first letter to her. She treats people with respect, and she deserves a great deal of respect for unapologetically touting the value of women's work.

Stephanie Pearl-McPhee also deserves my praise and gratitude. The best-selling author was inundated with demands on her time during the year that I wrote my book, and yet she made time for me.

Sabrina Gschwantdner helped me immensely to understand the realm of fine fiber arts. A fine artist and a curator herself, she took a leap of faith in sharing her time and knowledge with me. I was fortunate to meet her and learn from her.

Freddie Robins is English, but she fascinates knitters in America and around the globe, and I believe her influence on the way knitting is viewed will be substantial. I am very thankful that she was willing to contribute her thoughts and image to this book.

Many other women and men gave me their time, trust, and knowledge, and I am glad for all of their help. Brenda Dayne, Jesse Loesberg, Selma Miriam, Kay Gardiner, Rachael Herron, Zabet Stewart, Renée Rigdon, Kate Gilbert, Katie Franceschi, and Cat Mazza are among those I want to thank for sharing their stories with me. There are many other knitters who also deserve my thanks. I hope that acknowledgments in the form of notes will suffice to let you know how much I appreciate you.

I offer deep thanks to Hilary Claggett, who believed in this project, adopted it, and persuaded others at Praeger that it was worthy of their subculture series.

Lisa Pierce Breunig is my dear friend who recognized the story I had to tell. She picked up on my intense enthusiasm for knitting and absorption with the simultaneously ethereal and solid network of knitters around the world, through blogging. I never would have had the gumption to consider this endeavor without her confidence in me. I think women should make a more deliberate effort to acknowledge the support they get from other women, and so, I will lead by example and give Lisa her due credit and praise for believing in me.

I want also to thank my husband, Jonathan Wills, for his extreme patience and lovingness. Writing this book meant turning down freelance writing assignments, foregoing a full-time job that might have offered us money and benefits, and spending countless hours on research and writing when I might have been spending it with him in this, our second year of marriage. Jon, you are my love, my best friend, and my booster. I managed to live thirty-four years without you, but I do not know how.

And last, I must thank Meredith Wills-Davey, Jonathan's sister and my sister-in-law, for teaching me how to knit. This book never would have happened if she hadn't gotten the notion to sit me down with a pair of needles and some yarn. Meredith, you showed me that so-called domestic crafts do not diminish a person, even if she is an astrophysicist. Knitting is yet another of your many great accomplishments, and I am proud to say it is one of mine, too.

ABBREVIATIONS

BBC   British Broadcasting Company

CMU   Carnegie Mellon University

CYCA   Craft Yarn Council of America

DIY   do it yourself

EPS   Elizabeth's Percentage System

FIRE   Flagstaff International Relief Effort

FO   finished object

IRO   international rock-on symbol

KIP   knitting in public

KPC   Kunzang Palyul Choling, a Buddhist community

LYS   local yarn store

MAD   Museum of Arts and Design, New York City, New York

MSF   Medicins San Frontieres, French for Doctors Without Borders

NARAL   National Abortion and Reproductive Rights Action League

OFA   Orphan Foundation of America

PDA   personal digital assistant

PICA   Peace through Inter-American Community Action

RSS   several different terms, among them, "really simple syndication," "rich site summary," and "RDF site summary," all of which represent file formats that allow Web sites, web blogs, and podcasts to syndicate.

SABLE   Stash Accumulation Beyond Life Expectancy

SARS   Severe Acute Respiratory Syndrome

TGKA   The Knitting Guild of America

UFO   unfinished object

WIP   work in progress

INTRODUCTION

As I write this book, we are in the midst of an explosion in the popularity of knitting. Begun right around the start of the twenty-first century, this trend keeps growing, even as participants imagine it could not get bigger, or, perhaps, wish that it wouldn't. Because today's knitter frequently bucks the traditional stereotype of what a knitter should be, outsiders to this trend may look upon it as droll and short-lived. When did knitting become attractive to young people with nose rings and tattoos? When did third-wave feminists start posting photos of their knitted works in progress (WIPs that is) online? Why are books and online magazines for knitters publishing patterns for iPod cozies, yoga mat bags, and Joey Ramone dolls? And when did men start knitting? The cynical among us may assume that, ten years hence, many of these new knitters will cram their yarns, needles, and more eccentric projects into the back of a closet, next to the razor scooter and the bread machine.

Perhaps. Every hobby attracts some people with just a passing interest. Knitting, however, is likely to have a more enduring appeal for the latest generation of enthusiasts. Anyone who manages to overcome the initial frustration of learning the basic knit stitch knows that it is a peculiarly addictive motion. Like bicycling, knitting is a skill never truly forgotten. And like all habits, be they chocolate, gin, or heroin, yarn and needles are extremely difficult to put down.

Beyond the pleasure of the craft is the usefulness of it. An addiction to chocolate, gin, or heroin tends to waste time, one's body, and relationships. Knitting does the opposite. It makes fantastic use of spare moments and long stretches of erstwhile idleness. It keeps the mind simultaneously sharp and relaxed. And, since its beginnings, knitting has been a pretext for pulling people together, either for companionship or for particular causes. The usefulness of knitting extends far beyond that of the stockings, scarves, ponchos, or laptop covers produced. Because it is a kind of social glue, knitting will endure beyond every trend.

Many of us harbor an image of the knitter as a grandmother in a rocking chair, swathed in afghans of her own making. Grandmothers are a real and treasured segment of the knitting community, but they have never represented the entire subculture. Knitting has long been a way for women to express passions, political stands, and individuality. Like the confines of a particular poetic form, constraint to the realm of domesticity motivated women in prior ages to find creative ways to contribute to the social discourse, and often they did so through the use of their knitting needles.

My sister-in-law Meredith, an astrophysicist and avid knitter, was the first of many people to tell me that the current knitting fad is nothing new. Knitting, she said, enjoys a revived popularity every twenty years or so. She told me this as she taught me to knit, scarcely two years before I finished this book. I was sitting on the floor of her sewing room in uncomfortable, body-shaping undergarments and nothing else, struggling to understand where to insert my right needle and how to pull a knitted loop onto it. This frustrating and somewhat humiliating exercise was supposed to occupy me while Meredith sewed together a patchwork of scrap fabric to replicate the shape of the wedding dress she would make for me. I was her breathing mannequin, so I needed to stay nearby in my skivvies all afternoon.

As I struggled with my task for hours—this is no exaggeration—with no results beyond a string of knots, Meredith interjected, "I think you must be assuming this is harder than it really is. Grandmothers can do this. Children can do it." I burst into tears.

You'd think I would have dropped the needles and abandoned knitting for good. That was August of 2004. Since then, I have knitted about thirty items—hats, sweaters, scarves, toys, even a bed for my friend's kitten. I have taught myself Aran stitching to make a tiny cardigan for my future child, or children. I have hoarded yarns with no particular concern for how I will use them, just to expand my color palate and spur my imagination. I have joined what I believe is a never-ending circle of knitters—young and old, modern and traditional, rich and poor, multiracial, gay and straight. I have met on Philadelphia's funky South Street with a diverse group of knitters led by a former exotic dancer. I visit intermittently with a circle of knitters bound by their devotion to a political stance, the right of women to choose abortion. I get to know knitters around the globe through online rings that connect me to knitting blogs. I gleefully explore the yarn shops that seem to be sprouting up all over Pennsylvania, my new home, and Connecticut, my former home of fifteen years. I feed my delicious new obsession with books, magazines, and patterns.

Meredith despairs that people might think she is part of this knitting craze. She has been knitting for most of her life. I suspect that many of today's trendy knitters will join the ranks of tomorrow's old guard. Just as each generation's modern music eventually gets labeled "classic," today's knitting patterns will one day be rediscovered by future knitters who will call our cutting-edge styles, "vintage," or "retro," or whatever new term they invent for "cool because it's old-fashioned." And, if I'm lucky enough to get old, perhaps I will one day be the grandmother who passes down stitches and tips. I hope, by then, stereotypes about knitters will be old news.

One thing that quickly became apparent to me as I researched this book is that knitters are a heterogeneous group. Generalizations are wasted upon them. At first, I tried to get knitters to identify a single thing that they all had in common. Many interview subjects were stumped and even irritated by that request. The lack of a common trait among all knitters frustrated me as I tried to develop theses about the origins of the current knitting movement. Could I even call it a movement? No, I could not. Some people who picked up the hobby in recent years were just doing it for recreation. They were not devoted to or even aware of the political and social motivations that inspired people on the cutting edge of the trend.

Here's one example of a generalization that didn't apply to me. I am a knitter and a feminist. Several knitters I interviewed for this book noted how women my age (in their twenties and thirties) watched knitting skip a generation. Few of us had mothers or even grandmothers who taught us to knit. Our mothers had no time to knit; they were too busy defying the rules about what a woman could be. They were becoming doctors, scientists, and senators. Further, they rejected knitting because it was steeped in feminine associations. Knitting in public might have held them back.

This was not true of my mother. She knitted, crocheted, sewed, and embroidered. She was never a feminist. She was a cheerleader. She was blond, buxom, and beloved at Ridgefield High School, in an affluent Connecticut suburb. My mother was an average student, but popular. She loved folk music and the Kennedys. She often tells the story of how once, when she was a student at Boston University, the president's motorcade passed and John F. Kennedy waved to her. She was flush with idealism at age nineteen. And then, she got pregnant.

My mother's parents pulled her out of college but hid their embarrassment by sending her back up to Boston in the fall, long before she started to "show." They put her in a home for unwed mothers. Her own mother did not visit her there. Later, my mom would equate this place to a prison. To kill time, she would do crafts. She crocheted a pink bunny for her future baby. She didn't know if it would be a boy or a girl. When the child was born and turned out to be a boy, she named him Daryn. Then she handed him off to the state with his pink bunny, and she thought she would never see him again.

My mother never taught me to knit. I asked her to, but, after I had a few failed tries, she lost patience with me. I long assumed that it was just too hard, like all the other things I couldn't do: play piano, dance ballet, keep off weight, curl my hair. I figured these things weren't in my nature until, at thirty-six, I became a knitting dynamo.

My mother resented that an in-law tried to teach me what she could not. I explained that I had failed for hours with Meredith before consulting a book and getting the hang of it, but this didn't really appease my mother. She overcompensated at Christmas by knitting gifts for my two sisters and giving me twenty skeins of a yarn that didn't really speak to me, along with instructions for a long sweater coat in seed stitch that I didn't want to knit. Every two months or so we'd speak on the phone and she would ask, "Did you knit that coat?"

"Not yet," I'd tell her.

In 2005, my mother embarked on a search for Daryn. She expected it to be harder than it was. Daryn, whose name turned out to be David Mills, was looking for her, too. They found each other in short order, with help from Connecticut's state Department of Children and Families. David was happy to hear from my mother and eager to meet her. He was successful in his work, married, and the father of four children. Suddenly, my mother was a grandmother.

When you welcome a new brother into your family, you also invite a flood of emotions. You reassess your relationships with the family members you have known all your life. You compare your life to his. You think about your family's successes and shortcomings. You judge. You feel guilty, selfish, and ashamed for judging. If you are me, you hold your tongue and you knit.

No doubt, my new brother was going through a whole slew of emotions himself. But he didn't keep his mouth shut. He admitted his nervousness. He showed us pictures of his family. He answered questions about his life honestly. And then, he pulled out his pink bunny. He said, as a child, he knew the bunny came with him from the adoption agency, and he slept with it every night.

The rabbit was crocheted, not knitted, which is inconvenient as I try to wrap up this introduction to a book about the subculture of young American knitters. Any hopes I had of neat conclusions are foiled. What can I say? Life is messy. For some, knitting is a way to cope with that messiness. For others, maybe knitting is not the answer. Let us not invest this hobby with too much meaning. Clearly, for my mother, the answer was crochet.

1

A BRIEF HISTORY OF THE KNITTING WORLD

What I have compiled in this chapter owes much to modern historians. I am not a historian. My intent in writing a chapter on knitting history is to provide a context in which the current knitting revival can be properly understood. The ongoing knitting renaissance is truly unprecedented and remarkably different, and one can only fully grasp this by looking at the place of knitting in people's lives before today. I also strove to keep this history relatively brief, consolidating the salient facts from a handful of major academic sources and peppering the story with interesting tidbits from other places. Brevity commanded that I leave out many details. Those who are deeply intrigued by the finer points of history are heartily encouraged to read the titles listed in the notes. What follows is a somewhat focused and occasionally even personal glimpse into knitting's past.

I recall the first time I succeeded in creating a few rows of knitted fabric; it seemed like magic. The fact that one can take some yarn and two sticks and create with them sweaters, bags, hats, toys—any soft thing you can imagine—is part of knitting's allure. One might think that a phenomenon so delightful would inspire more documentation than it has.

Unfortunately, we know little about the origins and early history of this ancient craft. This dearth of information results in part from the tendency of traditional historians to concentrate on documenting the acts of people in power. No one ever knitted his way to a throne, knitted a lethal weapon, or knitted a constitution. And while knitting was for several centuries a valuable source of clothing and income to many people, those people were neither rich nor powerful. Even when knitting became popular with the affluent, as it did in Victorian England, women comprised the majority of its practitioners. Women's traditional contributions to society are routinely granted less importance than those of men. I specify "traditional contributions" because women who lead extraordinary lives by anyone's standards sometimes get their due. Consider Marie Curie, Queen Elizabeth I of England, Helen Keller, or Joan of Arc. Conversely, men who decide to perform a traditionally female activity, like knitting, often receive a flood of attention and either praise or suspicion, regardless of the quality of their work.

In her classic *A Treasury of Knitting Patterns*, Barbara Walker notes that knitting was long a male-dominated craft.[1] We don't know enough about the early years to really say that. And yet, it is true that Europe's knitting guilds, which originated during the Middle Ages in France and produced the masters who created garments, tapestries, and other knitted treasures for royalty, were exclusively male. At the same time, nuns living in poverty and seclusion likely created the exquisite knitted liturgical gloves that the clergy wore. Perhaps it is safer to say that lucrative knitting was the sole domain of men for most of history.

A FRAGMENTED PAST

Another reason for the craft's uncertain beginnings is that knitted fabric tends to rot. Our lack of knitted artifacts prevents us from knowing exactly when and where knitting was invented. Historian Richard Rutt conservatively suggests that the technique could have originated in Egypt sometime between 500 and 1200 A.D.[2] His estimate contradicts a commonly held but unconfirmed view among historians and laymen alike that knitting originated in Arabia.

In *A History of Hand Knitting*, Rutt determined that the oldest confirmed piece of knitting came from medieval Islamic Egypt. The scrap of knitting belonged to Swiss textile expert Franz Iklé (1877–1946), who dated it to the seventh to ninth centuries and claimed it was found at Fustat, the administrative capital of Egypt during the Middle Ages. Rutt suggested that the piece, now lost and unavailable for examination, might have been even newer.

Older fragments of apparent knitting have been discovered but were destroyed, either by time or the examination process, so that we can no longer confirm that they were knitted. Confusion occurs because so many early forms of fabric that resemble knitting were actually made by some other process. Rutt postulated that the oldest pieces of fabric claimed to have been hand knitting were more likely created by other methods. One way of creating looped fabric with a single needle, called nalbinding or knotless netting, can result in a fabric nearly identical to knitting.

Irena Turnau, a Polish historian of European textiles who spent years examining such relics throughout Europe, noted her great difficulty in telling the difference between ancient works of knitting and knotless netting. Most pieces were available for viewing only under glass and, often, in poor lighting. She proposed any of the fragments might, given closer examination, turn out to be made by another technique than knitting.[3]

Rutt suggests that Egyptians might have originated knitting to save time and energy, adapting the more labor-intensive work of nalbinding (what Turnau calls knotless knitting). Egyptians usually knit in the round to make footwear, although they could also knit flat pieces and knew how to knit more than one color into a row, a process we call intarsia today.

Nalbinding is more time-consuming than knitting and requires special dexterity, but it produces a smoother, denser, and more durable fabric than knitting does. Turnau notes that, when the quality of the fabric is valued more than the time required to produce it, some cultures still use nalbinding. Scandinavians in cold, mountainous regions use nalbinding to make extra-warm hats, gloves, and other hand and head garments, and Iranians continue to make footwear by nalbinding.

Over the years, other scraps of material have contended for the title of first knitted fabric. Two bits of cloth found in a woman's grave in Esch, southern Holland, were once widely thought to be the oldest examples of knitting, dating back to the late second century. And yet, scholars disagree about how the pieces were made. The pair of two-centimeter squares appeared to be a woolen yarn in stockinette stitch, mounted to another material—possibly leather. Two bronze rods were found in a box next to the squares of fabric.

Three pieces of fabric excavated from the ancient Babylonian city of Dura are also subjects of some debate. Dura, on the banks of the Euphrates River, was a border post between Syria and Mesopotamia and a stopping point for East-to-West traders. Sasanian Persians obliterated Dura in 246 A.D. An excavation in 1922 uncovered a third-century church, among other cultural riches. In 1933 Rudolf Pfister discovered the Dura fragments, which are now at the Yale University Art Gallery. Again, experts argue over whether the Dura fragments are really knitted. Furthermore, these three scraps present more mystery than usual because Dura was a trading center whose relics could have been created anywhere along East-West trading routes. The origins of the Dura fragments are anybody's guess.

FANCY NOTIONS

Many myths exist regarding knitting's history. Among these romantic but false notions is a story that the seamless shift worn by Jesus Christ, for which Roman soldiers cast lots before his crucifixion, was knitted. Rutt, former bishop of Leicester, argued that the seamless garment, called a khiton, was more probably woven. It was a rectangular piece of fabric that was wrapped around the body and pinned above one or both shoulders. Sometimes this shift was left open; other times it was belted. In either case, it would have been a single, seamless piece of fabric.[4]

Another fanciful idea is that Jesus' mother Mary knitted. In the fourteenth century, several painters depicted her in the act, sometimes negotiating with numerous bobbins and double-pointed needles. Rutt noted how these paintings were made during a period when the human and emotional aspects of Jesus' life became important to artists and writers in Northern Italy, such as Ambroglio Lorenzetti (ca. 1345) of Siena, Vitale degli Equi of Bologna (1308–1359), and Tommaso da Modena (1325–1375). Paintings of Jesus' mother knitting were part of a movement that portrayed the Holy Family in domestic settings that had no basis in the Bible. These paintings merely tell us that the artists knew about knitting before 1350 and that women might have knitted in the home at the time the paintings were made.

HAND IN GLOVE

In spite of those confusing paintings of a knitting Virgin Mary, historians have good reason to thank the Roman Catholic Church for preserving knitting history. We know knitting was widespread in Europe and England during the Middle Ages because the Catholic Church inventoried knitted liturgical gloves, which were commonly worn by bishops. Priests, too, wore these richly ornamented gloves, but theirs were usually made of sewn cloth or leather. The knitted ones were made of silk, wool, or less often, linen, and were white and sometimes red or purple. About thirty pairs of knitted gloves from the Middle Ages are preserved in church treasuries in Europe. Other evidence of the gloves abounds, including depictions of them in paintings and sculptures and references to them in literature.[5]

Turnau notes that these gloves, which clergy wore with secular clothing, too, say a lot about the role of knitting during the era. Shaping the five fingers would have required the gloves' knitters to be skillful. Turnau says that the glove knitters may have been nuns. One can imagine them in their convents, painstakingly manipulating tiny needles to make these elaborate and impressive symbols of clerical power.

Gloves, according to Turnau, had great cultural significance. Beyond power, gloves signified grace, dignity, and emotion in the wearer. Several traditions revolved around them. A gift of gloves could represent the end of a contract. A knight who was given a glove from a lady was obligated to protect her. A glove thrown to the ground was a gesture meant to provoke a fight or contest. As would be the case throughout much of history, the knitters were anonymous, but the wearers of the knitted product were people of means.

KNITTING AS AN INDUSTRY IN ENGLAND AND EUROPE

We think of knitting as a leisurely activity today, but initially, most people knitted out of necessity, either to clothe their own families or to make money. In England, caps were the first articles knitted for profit, as early as the thirteenth century. In Coventry, cappers, that is knitters of caps, were established by 1424.[6] Capper was a surname for some: Joan and Isabella Capper applied for licenses to sell caps in 1478. Turnau cites a knitters' guild in Paris, France as early as 1268, one in Tournai, Belgium in 1429, and in Barcelona, Spain in 1496. Knitters in other European cities may have worked in joint guilds. Only men were allowed guild membership. Meanwhile, women likely knit for their families without belonging to guilds, and nuns may have knit for the clergy. Head and hand coverings were the main garments knitted for sale in Europe. Turnau notes that in the European Continent, only Switzerland has examples of knit stockings from the Middle Ages.

Making three-dimensional objects like hats, gloves, and stockings required mastery of knitting with more than two needles—usually four or five of them. Turnau identifies this technique as the first technical upheaval in European knitting. It allowed all kinds of knitted garments to become popular and widely available in the thirteenth century.

Europe's Guilded Era of Knitting

Though most historical records of hand knitting in Europe come from guilds, Turnau describes how the adaptability of the craft would have made it a convenient home, farm, and convent activity. Because knitting is portable and can be done in short spurts, either between or during performance of other tasks, farm wives, shepherds, and itinerant workers could easily fit it into their workloads. Turnau, writing from within the former Eastern Bloc shortly after the fall of the Berlin wall, said that knitting's adaptability made it a common way to exploit laborers during the birth of capitalism in Europe. Orphans, convicts, soldiers, and people in forced labor institutions were assigned knitting, she wrote.[7]

Historians commonly hold that knitting skills made their way from the Middle East to Europe, primarily through Italy and Spain, but Turnau notes that little documentation backs these assumptions. Records do exist showing that costly silk stockings in a wide range of colors were exported from Toledo to the French court during the sixteenth century. Very little is known about knitting's origins in Italy, though knitting was exported from Milan, Genoa, Naples, and Mantua according to Turnau.

France was also a major knitting center in the sixteenth century. In 1514, the Parisian knitters' guild was one of the city's Six Corps—the most important guilds. Champagne was also a knitting center where guild members produced caps and stockings, Turnau wrote. Several other towns had knitting guilds, but the one that has sparked the most interest among historians is Dourdan, where machine production later took a stronghold. Silk articles were first knitted in Dourdan around the end of the sixteenth century. By 1650, a nun named Marie Poussepin, founder of the Dominican Sisters of the Presentation in Tours, set up a factory in Dourdan, where orphans aged six to twelve were set to work without pay knitting silk garments.[8] Turnau cites this as the beginning of manufacture based on forced labor in Europe.

The Catholic Church describes the nun's legacy differently. Historical information compiled by the Dominican Sisters of the Presentation and published on their Web site says that in 1683, at age thirty, Poussepin made "a bold and progressive move," in buying knitting machines to save the failing business that her father left behind after his death. The nuns claim Poussepin hired and trained apprentices treating them with, "a sense of social justice and with a Christian Charity [sic] well ahead of the practice of her time."[9]

Knitting guilds existed in other parts of Europe as well as France. Strasburg had one by 1535, and Prague formed one in 1570.[10] The Strasburg guild was a strong one. Even before the guild's formation, in the fifteenth century, Strasburg was home to about fifty knitting workshops. In 1598, at least 200 master knitters were represented at a discussion of guild regulations for Alsace and Switzerland, as well as in regions around Strasburg and Basel. In Strasburg, the guild controlled professional hand knitting until about 1700, when nonguild, hand-knitting competitors and French machine knitters significantly cut into their profits.

Stockings: A Cottage Industry in England

Though the home hand knitting industry got a later start in England than it did in the rest of Europe, English knitters dominated the knitted stocking market by the seventeenth century.

It wasn't until the reign of Queen Elizabeth I (1558–1603) that knitting became widely popular in England. This was in part because weaving was common, and most stockings, hats and other garments could be made of woven material. Also, slim knitting needles would have been difficult for a smith to make. It was only when a method was devised to draw steel through holes in plates that needles could be more easily produced.[11]

Stockings were the main item that people knitted in England. For the most part, only children wore stockings until Elizabeth's reign, when they became fashionable for men and women of every class to wear. As we shall see, though, English stockings would eventually be in great demand all over Europe.

As stockings became the rage, so did knitting become a common way for working-class families to generate income. All over England, farmers' families were knitting stockings for export to Germany, France, Holland, and Spain. Knitting was seen as a useful skill to teach to the poor, and knitting schools were formed in both cities and rural communities in Elizabethan days. By the end of the sixteenth century, about 200,000 hand knitters were generating roughly 20 million pairs of stockings annually in their homes,[12] making England the world's leading producer of knitted stockings. It is no wonder that the knitting frame, invented by William Lee sometime between 1589 and 1600, was not initially popular in England.

Lee got the idea for his knitting machine by watching his wife knit stockings in the round. Historians give varying accounts of Lee's motives. Some say that, during the couple's wedding engagement, Lee found his fiancée's knitting to be annoying because it took courtship time away from him. Others say that Lee felt pity for her and wanted to decrease her labors. Once married, though, Lee is said to have appreciated the income his wife's handicraft generated.

Queen Elizabeth rejected Lee's patent request based on the fiscal harm she believed the knitting frame would do to rural knitters throughout England. "I have too much love for my poor people who gain their bread by the employment of knitting to give my money to forward an invention that will tend to their ruin by depriving them of employment and making them beggars," she argued.[13] Exporting knitting frames from England was outlawed and subject to a fine.

FRANCE ADOPTS MACHINE KNITTING

After his invention failed to gain traction in England, William Lee moved to France. Lee worked on perfecting his machine so that it could knit silk stockings, not just woolen ones. By 1611, Lee partnered with several Frenchmen to open a factory in Rouen, making wool and silk stockings. Little else is known about Lee or his factory, except that he died, probably in Rouen, a few years after the factory opened. The French adopted Lee's invention far more readily than the English. By 1785, about 45,000 knitting machines existed in France—twice as many as in England. French machine knitting would substantially diminish the power of European hand knitting guilds by the eighteenth century. And while many of England's farm families would continue to earn money by hand knitting, the country would relinquish its dominance in the stocking industry by about 1750.

KNITTING IN OTHER PARTS OF EUROPE AND RUSSIA

Knitting became widespread in Scandinavia during the sixteenth century. The marshy land provided ample grazing for sheep, which supplied plenty of wool for knitting. Men and women of every age knitted all kinds of articles. Finland's knitting history is especially long. Nuns knitted stockings and mittens in a convent in Nadenal as early as 1438, according to Turnau. Finns took up knotless knitting, or nalbinding, in prehistoric times.

Knitting reached Iceland by the first half of the sixteenth century, when it was introduced either by English, German, or Dutch merchants. It wasn't until 1700 that hand knitting developed as a trade in Switzerland. Knitting also developed later in Slovakia and Hungary because men in those countries didn't need stockings; they wore longer garments and high boots, which covered their legs. Slovakia had a guild by the seventeenth century, and Hungary, by the eighteenth century. In each country, the rise in hand knittting coincided with the need for stockings, as men in eastern Europe began adopting Western styles of dress.

Little is known about the origins of hand knitting in Germany. Turnau says Frankfurt might have formed a knitting guild by the end of the sixteenth century, while in Saxony, knitters got started in the trade earlier. Dresden registered its knitters' guild statute in 1563 Berlin didn't start up a knitters' guild until machine knitting was underway. Even so, the German guild required master knitters to be able to make hand knitted articles, including the most difficult masterpiece, a multicolored carpet. Records show that many knitted stockings were imported from Italy and England at that time. In Poland, the formation of a knitting guild in 1620 in Gdansk also coincided with machine knitting. Turnau notes how guild members complained about competition from nonguild-affiliated knitters in the suburbs.

As early as 1661, a survey shows that guild members launched complaints against Jews, accusing Jewish knitters of refusing to contribute to the church order and not complying with guild and city rules.[14] Knitting guilds existed in Europe until the eighteenth century, when framework knitters became more prevalent.

Turnau also says that many knitting guilds were registered in parts of Russia that formerly belonged to the Polish Republic, including Ukraine and Lithuania. Dating the beginnings of hand knitting is difficult in other parts of Russia, as well as in eastern and northern Europe, where guilds did not exist. Turnau says the first mention of a knitter in Russia is from 1576 to 1580, in the records of a Russian Orthodox convent. Some of the oldest knitting discovered in Russia dates from the late sixteenth or early seventeenth century and came from the excavation of an island, Fadeev, in the eastern Siberian Sea.

Knitting was not common in Russia until the seventeenth century because, until then, men wore long robes modeled after those of the Far East, which did not require stockings. Women's clothing featured more knitwear as women were more likely to follow Western fashion. Turnau says that the tsars' court wore silk stockings by the seventeenth century, but these were probably imported from Europe. Russian Orthodox clergy eventually adopted liturgical gloves, as in Europe, and gloves were eventually part of the Russian military uniform. By about 1630, the military wore stockings, and in 1633, the military placed an order for knee-high stockings so large that Moscow's hand knitters could not outfit the regiments by themselves. Knitters in other Russian towns had to pitch in.

Turnau says that scant knowledge of hand knitting history exists in Russia because knitters weren't organized by major guilds, which might have documented the work. Turnau notes that women probably performed most knitting. She goes on to describe how, in the sixteenth and seventeenth centuries in Russia, the textile industry made ample use of production methods that required minimal skill but much labor. She cites Russian embroidery as an example of how women were exploited by the textile industry. "Young serf girls or nuns would laboriously imitate by hand the complicated patterns of imported velvets or brocades," Turnau wrote. "They covered extensive cloth surfaces with embroidery; and very often, after arduous toil, they would lose their sight."[15]

KNITTING IN EAST ASIA

The origins of knitting in the Western World are vague, but information on the birth of this craft in East Asian nations is foggier still.

Very few sources of history are available, and, as in the West, Eastern historians struggle to distinguish actual knitting from related forms of fabric-making that probably existed earlier. In all likelihood, knowledge of knitting arrived in Asia with European explorers.

The New China News Agency in Peking reported in 1983 that braids with a knitted structure were among textiles found in the tomb of a third-century noblewoman. Rutt said descriptions of the braids were not available in Europe as he wrote, and they may not have been knitted at all. By 1932, knitting was fairly common in China, though. That was when the yarn company Patons opened a mill in Shanghai.[16]

Knit Japan, a Web site based in the United Kingdom and devoted to highlighting Japanese knitting in English-speaking countries, offers a brief history of knitting in Japan. This was my source for what little I am able to provide here.[17]

The first Europeans to visit Japan arrived accidentally in 1542, when a Portuguese ship bound for China was blown ashore. Europeans would have worn stockings and other knitted items during their regular travels to Japan during the Azuchimomoyama period (1563–1598), but no evidence demonstrates that knitting technique was passed on to the Japanese during that era. From 1603 to 1867, during what is known as the Edo period, Japan cut off trading with the West. Some trading continued with the Dutch and the Chinese through Nagasaki, though, allowing for knitted items and, possibly, knitting technique to reach the Japanese.

Haiku from the Edo period includes the word "Meriyasu," which remains the Japanese word for stockinette stitch. Meriyasu is believed to have originated from the Spanish word for the same technique, which is "Medias," or from the Portuguese word, "Meias." Some speculate that Nagasaki prostitutes learned to knit from their European clients.

Japan's oldest examples of knitting are in the Suifumyotokukai Syokokan museum in Mito City. They include seven pairs of stockings, probably knitted outside of Japan, and owned by Mitokomon-Mitukuni Tokugawa (1628–1700), who was the grandson of Ieyasu Tokugawa, the first Shogun of Japan.

Knitting appears to have flourished in Japan only at the end of the Edo period. In 1853, American Commodore Matthew Perry sailed with four warships into Japan's Yedo Bay, now Tokyo, bearing a letter from U.S. President Millard Fillmore, requesting that Japan reopen its borders. Perry returned the following year to witness the signing of "Agreements for Friendly Relations between the United States and Japan," known in the United States as the Treaty of Kanagawa.[18]

The signing of that document introduced dramatic changes to Japan's government and military, though officially, the Edo period did not end until 1867. For one thing, the samurai warrior class, which had long enforced Shogun rule, saw its influence diminish. Japan's military was becoming more like those of the West, and they dressed like Western soldiers, too. Soon, knitted socks and gloves were in high demand. Remarkably, the samurai, now in need of income, took up needles and yarn themselves. They made money by knitting a Japanese style of sock called Tabi, which featured split toes. Knit Japan notes that one can see a reproduced illustration of a samurai knitting at the Sock Museum in Sakata, Japan.

KNITTING IN AMERICA

It wasn't until 1818, according to some historians, that a stocking machine was smuggled to North America in a shipment of salt. That date is questionable though; in 1771, *The Virginia Gazette* advertised, "a newly invented instrument for knitted, knotted, and double-looped work, to make Stockings, Britches Pieces, or Silk Gloves, Cotton or Worsted, together or separated."[19]

The Framework Knitters' Guild incorporated in 1657, but hand knitting continued for another two centuries as a common source of income for working-class people in England. Hand knitters could be more flexible to changing fashion than could early framework knitters. Investors were wary of the expense of setting up frames, while hand knitters on farms could cheaply fit knitting in between other tasks. Furthermore, knitting frames didn't always work that much faster than a pair of hands. Rutt wrote that a framework knitter might be able to make ten pairs of stockings a week, but an accomplished hand knitter could knit six. Frame knitters' speed could not outrun the productivity of hand knitters until about 1750. Most people also favored the quality of handmade stockings.

The economist Adam Smith noted in the fifth edition of *The Wealth of Nations* in 1789 that "Stockings in many parts of Scotland are knit much cheaper than they can anywhere be wrought upon the loom."[20]

Traders in the North American colonies were doing a brisk business in hand-knit British stockings, and the expense of knitting machines deterred many entrepreneurs from importing them. At the same time, colonial women were knitting scads of stockings, supplying those who couldn't afford British imports. The northern Philadelphia neighborhood of Germantown was a hotbed of knitting activity. Women there are reputed to have sold 60,000 pairs of stockings in 1759, "of their own make," which likely implies that they knit them by hand.[21]

The demand for stockings in the colonies was so great that local and even state governing bodies set up incentives and penalties to promote hand knitting. Some townships encouraged families to knit by offering bounties of a few shillings per pair produced, or by demanding quotas based on a family's headcount of women, boys and girls, as well as the family's other responsibilities and their knitting skill. A dozen pair of stockings knit from yarn grown in Virginia would garner a premium of ten pounds of tobacco. In Hatfield, Massachusetts, selectmen even imposed fines for noncompliance with family knitting quotas.

Male and female slaves also knit for the families of their owners. Sometimes slaves were allowed to sell their wares, if an owner deemed the plantation's needs had been met. Very little is written about hand knitting by slaves in America.

While the American colonies attempted to grow their textile market, England was fighting to preserve its own. England's Parliament imposed the 1699 Woolen Act, forbidding the transport of wool or woolen products among plantations in the American colonies, or to anywhere else. The order raised the ire of American settlers, who continued to sell their woolen wares at home and abroad.

British restrictions on trade in the American colonies, culminating with the Stamp Act of 1765, provoked the colonial spirit of rebellion that would lead to the American Revolution. Colonists boycotted British products and did their best to produce their own wares.

Women, who were shunted from direct political activism and discussion, were nonetheless eager to support the cause. Domestic productivity became their outlet, and knitting was one of the ways in which they contributed to the colonies' independence from England.

In her book *No Idle Hands: The Social History of American Knitting*, Anne L. Macdonald illuminates how, throughout American history and particularly in times of war, women have turned to knitting as a way to expand the boundaries of the domestic realm and contribute to political goals.

The first example of this domestic activism took place following England's establishment of the Stamp Act in 1765, which taxed colonists for a wide array of goods and services. It was England's first serious attempt to exert commercial and governmental control over the colonies, and it came when England was struggling under the weight of huge debt following the Seven Years' War. The Sons of Liberty, bands of colonists composed mostly of artisans and merchants, used violent protest to try to spur the resignation of English stamp distributors.[22]

Meanwhile an auxiliary group, The Daughters of Liberty, organized to spin yarn, knit, and weave fabric so that colonists might clothe themselves in hand-wrought garments and become less dependent on English imports. The Daughters turned domestic fabric production into a distinctly political act. Over the course of a year, knitting and spinning bees became extremely trendy in the colonies.

"Fierce competition between congregations, between married and unmarried women, between towns and cities and between old and young converted proceedings into such festive social occasions that hundreds of merry spectators milled around in the grounds, augmented in the evening by men who joined the spinners and knitters for picnics and boisterous Sons of Liberty ballads."[23]

Homemade clothing became commonplace, while the colonies' textile industry also grew in places like Germantown. The English continued to tighten their strictures on the colonies. As war approached, colonial leaders implored women to spin and knit even more, supplying clothing not only for their families, but also for soldiers. Congress assigned a Clothier General, who sought money for army supplies from the states. The states, in turn, applied to townships to garner funds and sometimes clothing for the soldiers. Responding to the call, spinners and knitters stepped up their productivity.

In Philadelphia, a city where knitting flourished, America's first large-scale women's association was formed, calling itself George Washington's Sewing Circle. This group overstepped the former bounds of women's political action by soliciting funds for the war effort, which members hoped the general's wife, Martha Washington, would distribute directly to soldiers at the front. The group's fundraising raised some consternation, both among husbands who worried about their wives' safety on the streets, and among people who found the women's vigorous approach distasteful. And yet, the association did raise the equivalent of $2 a man for the soldiers. When traveling between towns, these women were also likely to knit. One fundraiser from New Jersey who knitted during her travels to encourage others to knit for the war cause collected 133 pairs of stockings in a single week.[24]

At the end of the campaign, Martha Washington delivered the funds to her husband, who proposed either buying shirts or having the ladies make them. The club members balked, believing that shirts were necessities that ought to have been supplied by the states through Congress. They preferred to see the men receive the money directly, though some worried it would be spent on alcohol. In the end, their leader Sarah Franklin Bache, wife of Ben Franklin, encouraged the ladies to sew the shirts, 2,200 of them, each with the sewer's name attached to make the gift more personal.

Other women also worked to give comfort to soldiers. Some rode out to General George Washington's troops at the front, replenishing supplies of food and clothing and risking intervention from spies. Martha Washington frequently stayed with her husband at the camp at Valley Forge, Pennsylvania where a coterie of ladies would often join her for knitting and socializing. Another group of less high-stationed women also traveled with the troops, repairing their worn garments, cooking and knitting for them, and making love to them. Some criticized these women for getting in the way, but others attributed them with saving the spirits of the men.

A particularly interesting story was that of Old Mom Rinker, an eccentric woman who volunteered her spying skills to General Washington, stealing to him tidbits that she overheard at an inn owned by her relatives. Long before the days of James Bond and secrets stored on microfiche, Old Mom Rinker used balls of yarn to hide scraps of paper on which she wrote her information. She would station herself with her flax lying out to dry on a cliff near the camp. When the troops approached, she would surreptitiously nudge the yarn ball off the edge of the cliff, and the soldiers would grab it.[25]

Women in the United States would repeatedly lift their needles in support of soldiers during times of war. In the century after the American Revolution, women turned their attention to social reform. Ladies would knit for the poor or teach them to knit during the nineteenth century. Meanwhile, women's magazines like *Godey's Ladies' Book* extolled the virtues of womanhood and created a cult of domesticity, in which needlework of all kinds was upheld as ladylike behavior.

I took particular interest in one young woman's distaste for the way needle arts were heralded as appropriate feminine activities. In her intensely readable history, Macdonald singled out the following quote from a youthful Maria Mitchell, who would later be an astronomer (like my sister-in-law, Meredith) and the first woman inducted into the American Academy of Arts and Sciences. The quote was included in the 1973 collection, *Growing up Female in America*. Mitchell wrote in her diary:

> It seems to me that the needle is the chain of woman, and has fettered her more than the laws of the country. . . . I would as soon put a girl alone into a closet to meditate as give her only the society of her needle.[26]

Women continued to knit at home for profit in America. The same was true in England, although, by the end of the eighteenth century, rural hand knitting was on a downturn there. As pioneers in the American colonies packed into covered wagons to move out west, women knitted to pass idle time and ease loneliness. Their goods were especially valuable when they settled into new homes. Homesteaders decorated with knitted tablecloths, curtains, and bedspreads.

The Civil War prompted women at home to knit countless socks for soldiers, as those issued by the government quickly wore through. Soldiers' feet, unguarded by socks, would swell until their boots would not fit and they had to walk barefoot through the snow. Frostbite claimed toes, feet, and lives if gangrene set in. On the Union side, it became nearly impossible to deliver needed food and clothing directly from one home to a particular soldier. To expedite the process, the United States Sanitary Commission, precursor to the American Red Cross, was formed in 1861. Families were urged to knit for the agency, which forwarded goods to soldiers. Sometimes knitters would personalize their donations by writing encouraging poems or notes and either pinning them to garments or tucking them into socks and mittens.[27]

Southern women also knitted for Confederate soldiers. Initially, they too, tried to address their gifts of food and clothing to particular soldiers, but this proved too difficult. Instead, care packages were sent to a particular company, or, later in the war, to any Confederate Army soldiers. Women in the South also tried to hand-deliver some of their gifts to the front.

In 1855, a knitting machine for home use was patented, promising to replace the need to hand-knit stockings. The machine didn't sell very well, though. Generally, people considered handmade stockings to be of higher quality. Beyond that, women were simply reluctant to give up hand knitting. Other changes in gender roles affected the popularity of knitting. For instance, women took up sports that might require knitted garments. The bicycle craze of the 1890s required women to expose their legs and spurred sock knitting.

And yet, as the end of the nineteenth century approached, women were more likely to buy clothing than to knit it. The effects of the Industrial Revolution, begun as early as 1750 with changes in agricultural methods, were finally leading to a reduction in the amount of knitting women were likely to do. It's a funny turn of events, when you consider that sheep—the source of so much wooly knitting pleasure today—played a significant role in England's agricultural revolution.

By the end of the seventeenth century in England, serfdom had been replaced by tenancy among farmers. Wealthy landowners rented their large tracts of land to several farmers, who shared their produce. Rules prevented landlords from evicting tenants without cause, so that often families would farm the same land for generations.

All that changed during the years around 1750, when England's population surged to 5.7 million, leading to a need for more food, clothing, and other goods. The sudden demand for cloth made sheep farming more profitable. Though the population may have grown as large before, this was the first time when agricultural innovations allowed supply to accommodate demand. Landlords began to enclose pastures where sheep grazed and limit farmers' access to lands they had formerly used in common. Enclosure, combined with agricultural methods that increased productivity, forced farmers without property and women, who were deemed too frail to handle farm machinery, to find other ways to earn income. Meanwhile, the population was able to continue growing, and it reached 16.6 million by 1850.[28]

Academics disagree over how drastically enclosure affected farmers, depending on their political inclinations. Those on the political left claim enclosure and other agricultural innovations forced droves of farmers off the farms and into poverty. More conservative historians say enclosure's effect was less dramatic.

Development of cottage industries such as stocking knitting resulted. The importance of cottage hand knitting to England's economy, the quality of hand-knit stockings, and the many benefits attributed to hand knitting allowed the craft to prevail over the knitting machine for nearly two centuries.

At the start of the twentieth century, women were more likely to buy their clothing than to make it. And yet, marketers were still hailing knitting as a feminine skill and a virtuous sign of frugality in a homemaker. Suffragists were criticized as unattractive dressers, and, at times, their activism was attributed to nervousness or other mental defect. Again, knitting was urged as a way to calm their overwrought sensibilities.

War continued to be one of the great motivators for knitters, once clothing became cheaper and easier to buy than to make. Knitters answered the American Red Cross' call for socks, sweaters, knitted helmets, and other comforts to soldiers during World War I and World War II with the same fervor that Revolutionary and Civil War knitters brought to the task.

World War I saw men and children joining the women to contribute their skills. The Navy League sponsored a massive knitting bee in 1918, in New York City's Central Park, with contests, music, and food. Participants paid a fifty-cent fee to offset the cost of supplying wool to needy knitters. There, male knitters enjoyed the attention of onlookers and documenters of the event. Civil War veteran I. R. Seelye and police officer Patrick Fitzgibbons were among the men photographed contributing their skills with needles and yarn. Knitters swarmed to the park and raised $4,000, while donating 50 sweaters, 4 dozen mufflers, 224 pairs of socks, and 40 helmets. Many unfinished items were also promised upon their completion.[29]

The bee was just one example of citizens' generosity. The need was great during World War I, and the Red Cross put out an urgent plea for knitted garments and encouraged new knitters to use knitting machines, available at their headquarters, to quickly assemble socks for soldiers. Wealthy benefactors, such as John D. Rockefeller and Mrs. Joseph Pulitzer, opened up their homes to volunteers knitting for the war effort. Knitters across the nation assembled at formal teas and parties, and clubs that were once dedicated to sewing started knitting. Schools across the country and the American Red Cross taught countless children, both boys and girls, to knit for soldiers. And, when women did knit for themselves or their kin, they often whipped up smart, military-style fashions in khaki, navy, or brown, which demonstrated their patriotism. Simply carrying a knitting bag became a patriotic gesture.

BAA, BAA . . . BURNOUT

It's not surprising that, when peace finally came in 1919, many knitters put down their needles, suffering burnout. The American Red Cross was still hoping to encourage knitting for war refugees and was quick to remind tired knitters that peacetime offered the opportunity to knit in colors other than navy and khaki. On top of burnout, women were hearing the siren call of feminism urging them to seek their own careers.

Women were adopting higher hemlines and throwing out their corsets. Long hair was replaced by the bob, and makeup gained popularity. The curvaceous figures that were emphasized by clingy sweaters were going out of style, as flappers emaciated themselves and wore bust- and hip-reducing garments to achieve a pin-straight, boyish profile. New fashions that displayed more leg and décolletage and used less and filmier fabric, incited the old guard to push for dress reform. Many young people began to equate knitting with the old-fashioned, domestic role of women that they were trying to doff. Yarn producers tried to woo knitters with new bright colors and knitting contests with substantial cash prizes, but their efforts were of little avail. First Lady Grace Coolidge even attached her name to a national knitting contest sponsored by Fleisher Yarns in April 1923. Her advocacy of the contest, along with $11,000 in prize money, attracted several thousand knitters to enroll. Even so, the popularity of the craft continued to decline, as Mrs. Calvin Coolidge represented to many young women the very image of domesticity that they shunned.

One enterprising industrialist, Bernard Ulmann of Fleisher and Bear Brand yarns, entreated England's Princes Alfred and George to promote knitting for the sake of the Australian wool market. The beloved princes did one better, each knitting a scarf that their mother displayed in 1929 at Queen Mary's Needlecraft Guild.[30]

Rather than inspire hand knitting, the royal family spurred sales of British styled machine-knit fashions–sporty argyle sweaters and socks, and dignified tones of yellow, brown, and grey. The look was all the rage among affluent golf and tennis players and the country club set.

Mass production and wealth had caused women to trade knitting for shopping, but when the Great Depression struck, necessity led many to dig out their knitting needles again. A knitting craze ensued. Ulmann, the owner of Fleisher and Bear Brand yarns, urged the marketing of hand knitting as not only economical but fashionable as well. He and others in the industry courted the art needlework buyers for upscale stores with style shows in posh locales, such as New York City's Waldorf-Astoria Hotel.

Ulmann also saw the need to employ skilled hand knitters to demonstrate techniques and offer advice in stores, so that poorly made hand-knits wouldn't sink a knitting trend. While most full-time sales jobs still went to men, hundreds of women were able to work part-time and during peak sales periods. These sales workers included married women, who were more likely to have been unemployed before the Depression.

The marketing tactics worked: in 1935 yarn sales increased by 50 percent over the previous year. Yarn sales had doubled and sometimes even quadrupled over those of 1932, and, in spite of the nation's hard economic times, hundreds of small yarn shops opened.

Getting a job in a department store wasn't the only way for hand knitters to make money from the craze. Many women took the opportunity to teach their craft in their homes to friends and neighbors. Meanwhile, the yarn and fashion industries perpetuated the knitting renaissance in other ways. Colleges and public schools were urged to offer knitting as part of their adult education curriculums.

Magazine articles raved about knitting, with *Vogue* even claiming at one point that, "Knitting is no longer a fad, it's a national institution."[31] And, about seventy years before *Celebrity Scarves* featured photos of Daryl Hannah, Eartha Kitt, Julianna Margulies, Rosie Perez, and Rikki Lake,[32] the publisher Ulmann, Fleisher and Motion Picture Publications, Inc. exploited the stars with their title, *The Motion Picture Movie Classic Hand Knit Fashions as Worn by Warner Brothers Stars*. While the book made no claims that celebrities it featured knit their own clothes, it did purport that the hand knitter could dress like Bette Davis or Olivia de Havilland by following the patterns that accompanied the stars' photos. And, of course, the book included entry forms for a contest, into which knitters could submit their completed celebrity-style outfits, as long as they supplied the yarn bands to prove that they used the sponsor's brand. The grand prize was a trip to Hollywood, and other prizes were chosen to give winners the "star treatment"—a beaver coat, a pearl necklace, a bottle of perfume, among them. Eventually, magazines would indeed spread the word of celebrity knitters, like Joan Crawford and Katherine Hepburn. Yarn producers responded to the fad with an array of new fibers, textures, weights, and colors.

And every garment imaginable, from a full suit to a swimsuit, became fair game for knitters. We will look more at knitting among modern-day celebrities in a later chapter.

About 10 million Americans were knitting at the height of the trend. The thirties were when the phenomenon of knitting in public, which in recent years has acquired the acronym KIP among knitters, first aroused attention. The press commented on women knitting on trains and buses, in courtrooms and legislative halls, and during college classes. Men joined the craze, attending bees and even starting their own knitting clubs. Women still far outnumbered male knitters. Even so, knitting men of the thirties, just as today, enjoyed disproportionate attention—alternately in the forms of scorn and praise—for mastering what was generally considered a woman's craft.[33]

When Americans addressed their collective concern to World War II in 1939, knitters turned their enthusiasm toward making warm things for the military and civilians in Europe. Again, the Red Cross hosted volunteer knitters. Communities throughout the United States began "Knittin' for Britain," and four songs on that topic even made the record charts. The British Voluntary Organizations published *Knitting for the Army*, directions for knitting appropriate clothing for soldiers. Garments included cap mufflers, which replaced knitted helmets for wear under metal ones and allowed for removal of headphones, gloves without thumbs and forefingers, to aid shooting, and oiled socks that were more resistant to wetness.

By the time the United States entered the war in 1941, knitters had already begun making garments for reserve forces. They took to the task of knitting for the armed forces with their usual vigor. Items donated by knitters were always labeled as comforts rather than necessities, to avoid suggesting that the government provided inadequately for its soldiers. But the hand-knit sweaters, socks, hats, gloves, and other items were a great help to the fighting forces.

Interestingly, few knitters provided comforts for women in the military.[34] This lapse occurred despite obsessive national knitting for troops, enough to make civilian men complain of holes in their socks, to make cartoonists tease the trend, and to make at least one observer surmise that knitters for the war effort got at least as much joy out of their knitting—the high the habit gave them was similar to marijuana's, he proposed—as the soldiers got from donning the knitted gifts.[35]

Knitting clubs were very popular during World War II, which was when one such club coined the now pervasive phrase "Stitch and Bitch," according to Macdonald's research. The first discovered Stitch and Bitch Club was a group of a dozen women with children in Akron, Ohio, who moved in with their parents or in-laws when their husbands went to war. Once a week they would meet to knit, sew, snack, and, like gathered knitters everywhere, bitch. They met until each of their husbands returned from the war, except for one.[36]

The baby boom further fueled yarn sales. New patterns for baby's garments flooded the market in 1943, shortly after the announcement of National Baby Week. On top of that, a rubber shortage meant that elasticized legs and waists were no longer available for babies' waterproof underpants. Women began knitting cotton "soakers," which were very absorbent and could drain the moisture from a baby's diapers. Lots of soakers were needed, though, since they took several days to dry. Add to these projects the need for more and warmer clothing, due to fuel rations, and it's clear why women kept up their knitting so constantly.

Teens and college-aged women were continuing to knit, as shorter, clingier sweaters came into vogue. Movie actress Lana Turner's voluptuous figure is famous for its effect on sweater sales. Knitting continued to be popular in the 1950s, when yarn marketers successfully pitched argyle patterns, launching a four-year craze for the diamond-shaped color work on socks and sweaters.

The fifties were a time when domesticity was glorified as a high virtue for women. The uncertainties presented by World War II probably led many women to wed earlier than their mothers did, and fewer young women worked outside the home. Even so, knitting fell out of fashion after the passing of the argyle craze. Women lost interest in the craft, having felt compelled to knit constantly during wartime.

In 1963, feminist Betty Friedan published her landmark work, *The Feminine Mystique*, which identified a malaise among homemakers, "the problem that has no name."[37] Women across the nation were describing dissatisfaction with their homebound lives, noting their boredom, depression, anxiety, and fatigue. Friedan prescribed a cure of education and career, and her message struck a chord with millions of women.

Friedan and other feminists of the second wave, the first wave being suffragists, typically focused on empowering women to pursue traditionally male careers, to become doctors, lawyers, or engineers for instance. As women worked to gain credibility in those historically male spheres, they often abandoned or at least hid their interest in pursuits labeled as feminine.

Woe to the feminist who secretly enjoyed knitting. It would have been an embarrassment. Knitting was certain to evoke images of grandmothers, the home, and archaic feminine stereotypes. And sure enough, hand knitting suffered an even greater lull in popularity.

Even so, in the late seventies, a trio of middle-aged women spawned a renewed interest in the ancient craft. At the helm of this triumvirate was Elizabeth Zimmermann, whose plucky, opinionated demeanor and innovative and liberating knitting techniques showed that knitters did not have to be timid, dull, or passive. Knitting would fall out of fashion again in the eighties and for the first half of the nineties. Still, the modern revival of hand knitting owes much to Zimmermann.

KNIT IT LIKE ZIMMERMANN

Elizabeth Zimmermann was born Elizabeth Lloyd-Jones in England in 1910 and attended art schools in Switzerland and Germany. She married a German brewmaster named Arnold Zimmermann, and the pair immigrated to the United States before having children. Like many immigrants, the Zimmermanns first settled in New York City. That was where the couple had a daughter, Margaret, who today carries on Zimmermann's knitting legacy.

Meg Swansen, Elizabeth's youngest child, recalls in her book, *Meg Swansen's Knitting*, that her family moved to the artists' colony community of New Hope, Pennsylvania, where at age four or five, Elizabeth Zimmermann taught her daughter to knit.[38]

Even Swansen, today considered a legend of the knitting world, professes that she didn't knit much at all for about a decade through most of the fifties, until near the end of high school when she knitted a sweater for a boyfriend.

By that time, Swansen's family was living in Shorewood, Wisconsin. As Betty Friedan was researching *The Feminine Mystique*, Elizabeth Zimmermann was designing knitting patterns for magazines and devising a way to spread her philosophy of liberating knitters.

In the late fifties, *Vogue* commissioned Zimmermann to knit and draft the first set of instructions for an Aran sweater ever published in the United States. They were published in the *Vogue Pattern Book* of February/March 1957. Though she was excited about that coup, Zimmermann was also frustrated that other sweater patterns, which she designed using the knitting in the round technique, eliminating the need for sewing side seams, were routinely changed to accommodate flat knitting. She had strong opinions about knitting, and she wanted a forum for her ideas. According to Swansen, her mother arranged that, in lieu of payment, *Vogue* would cite her as the source for the wool used to make the Aran sweater. Zimmermann also started sending out newsletters with classic knitting patterns that used 100 percent wool yarn, a rarity in those days, and she began importing the precious fibers from Europe.

In 1959, Zimmermann officially launched Schoolhouse Press, a company devoted to promoting and selling pure wool and circular knitting needles, from her home in Shorewood. Later she recorded *Knitting*

Workshop, a series of instructional programs that aired on the Public Broadcasting System television.

"I'm going to make you work like mad," Zimmermann threatened, glaring down her nose and over the rims of her glasses. Viewers quickly learned that, despite her ominous British sternness, Zimmermann was bound to seem like a friend in their living rooms. She would challenge knitters to try new techniques that might have seemed difficult at first, but she would always explain her reasoning.

She wanted knitters to use the long-tail cast-on method, which was a bit tricky, but which was neater and saved one a row of knitting. She encouraged knitters to try knitting both English style, with the yarn in the right hand, and Continental style, where the yarn is held in the left hand. She rarely described methods that varied from hers as "wrong," even when explaining common errors. Zimmermann was more likely to demonstrate the result of the mistake and let viewers decide for themselves how they would proceed.

Among her great innovations was EPS, that is, Elizabeth's Percentage System. Zimmermann emboldened knitters to create sweaters without using patterns. Instead, the knitter could employ EPS, a series of proportions, to knit sweaters to fit their own bodies. This freed the knitter from the tyranny of magazine patterns sized to fit fashion models.

Zimmermann was an adamant defender of wool over the acrylic yarns that for a long time dominated the market. In her very first lesson on *Knitting Workshop*, Zimmermann described why she favored wool over all synthetic fibers.[39]

"It's pleasant, and it's beautiful, and it's warm, but it's a renewable resource," she said. "I don't want, when I burn my sweaters for them to go up in the air as smoke and come down as acid rain."

Unlike synthetics, which she noted "behave very strangely in the washing machine," wool, if washed carefully, "as you would wash a baby," will keep its form and last a lifetime she told her television audience.

"Wool is just a hair of a sheep, sweating in the spring, longing to have its coat sheared off so it can skip and gambol in the sunshine," Zimmermann said.

In 1974, Zimmermann led the nation's first knitting retreat at the University of Wisconsin extension at Shell Lake. This was the origin of Knitting Camp, an annual gathering of knitters that Swansen continues to this day at a hotel in Marshfield, Wisconsin.[40] Hundreds of knitters attend a series of sessions each summer, some of which are deliberately organized to be more reunions than learning events.

In a segment produced for Wisconsin Public Radio, Swansen said that many Knitting Camp attendees are true disciples of her mother, who died in 1999. "She was mesmerizing," Swansen said.

Barbara Walker also changed the way women looked at knitting during a time when it was not popular. She published a series of reference books filled with more than a thousand stitch patterns, the first being *A Treasury of Knitting Patterns* in 1968. The clear instructions and illustrations in these books vaulted them quickly to the status of classic knitting volumes.

Walker was born in 1930 in Philadelphia, Pennsylvania and later studied journalism at the University of Pennsylvania. She developed an interest in feminism while volunteering in the mid-seventies for a hotline for battered women and pregnant teenagers. In the eighties and onward, she published many books on topics such as women in relation to organized religion, mysticism, spirituality, and neo-Paganism. She identifies herself as an atheist, and her feminist writing often explores her belief in Neolithic matriarchies.

The third major influence on knitting during its less fashionable days was Mary Walker Phillips, who was among the first people to promote knitting as a fine art. Born in 1923, she grew up in Fresno, California and later studied at Cranbrook Academy of Art in Bloomfield Hills, Michigan. She began her career as a weaver in San Francisco in 1947. In 1949, she spent three weeks at Taliesen West, the Arizona home of architect Frank Lloyd Wright, where she designed woven pieces for the house. Walker Phillips returned to Cranbrook in 1960 to pursue a master of fine arts in experimental textiles and design. There, she began to view knitting as a medium capable of producing fine art. Upon graduating in 1963, she headed for New York City. Her seminal book is *Creative Knitting: A New Art Form*. Permanent collections of her work inhabit several major museums, including the Smithsonian Institution in Washington, D.C. and the Museum of Modern Art in New York.[41]

In Chapter 6, Art in the Craft, we will explore how modern fine artists have taken up the torch, moving beyond knitting as a design element and exploiting, even subverting, the genre to create works that are irrefutably fine art.

2

KNITTING MAKES A COMEBACK

Knitting is more popular than ever. The Craft Yarn Council of America (CYCA), the yarn industry's trade association, estimated in a 2004 consumer survey that one in every three American women, that is, 53 million women, know how to knit or crochet. The results were so surprising to the association that they broke their biennial survey tradition and commissioned another narrower survey in 2005, focusing more on consumer trends.

The first survey showed that women aged twenty-five to thirty-four led the knitting and crocheting renaissance. The second survey, conducted in 2005 by Research Incorporated of Atlanta, Georgia, showed that knitting and crocheting among those young women increased by 150 percent between 2002 and 2004—more than in any other age category. About 6.5 million—that's one in every three women aged twenty-five to thirty-four—started knitting or crocheting in those two years. Girls to age eighteen were the second fastest growing category of knitters and crocheters. Their ranks grew by 100 percent, from 8 percent to 16 percent of all girls in the age range, representing 5.7 million girls.

It happens that women aged 55 to 64 also increased their knitting from 2002 to 2004—by 74 percent, which represented 7.8 million women—but that trend didn't get the same media attention as the upswing in young knitters.

"I think the trend brought back many people who might have done it years ago," said CYCA's executive director, Mary Colucci.[1] "It certainly caught on with the twenty- to thirty-year-olds, because it's such a social thing."

Note also that the CYCA didn't survey yarn crafts among men at all. Older knitters probably garner less attention from marketers because they are the mainstay of the yarn industry. Yarn sellers count on this group's loyalty. Men, on the other hand, probably do not represent a large enough portion of the knitting population to attract the industry's interest.

In contrast, the surge in young female knitters was dramatic. Somewhere in the mid- to late nineties, women in their twenties and thirties, busy women with college educations, stressful careers, and family responsibilities, started to knit. Despite the many demands on their time, they chose a hobby that is time consuming. In an era when these women were more able than ever before to pursue historically male roles—becoming doctors, lawyers, scientists, business executives, professors—they opted to learn a traditionally female craft.

As counterintuitive as the knitting revival may seem, it is, for some of the young women leading the trend, a deliberate reaction to current aspects of women's modern lives. People interviewed for this book include knitting celebrities and pioneers of the current knitting movement as well as everyday knitters. Over and over, many described similar reasons for the popularity of the craft. Chief among these is a trait that has always attracted people to knitting: its restorative power. The repetitive motion of the needles is almost meditative. And, yes, the recent bevy of sumptuous fibers available on the market was often cited as a lure to knitting.

And yet, some larger forces than the lure of yarn and needles are feeding the current knitting craze. Remember that the upswing in knitting began among young women aged twenty-five to thirty-four. Interviews with women in this age group reveal that many of them are educated, possessing at least undergraduate college degrees. Many have jobs that traditionally have been held by men. I have met knitting engineers, architects, ministers, software designers, attorneys, and financial analysts. Many of these young, new knitters belong to the middle or upper middle class. Many also claim an alliance to one or both of two modern movements: the do-it-yourself (DIY) movement and third-wave feminism.

I stress that these movements were instigators of the knitting craze's avant-garde, not motivation for all modern knitters. Older, longtime knitters, as well as young ones, may not relate to or even know about either DIY or third-wave feminism. Even so, it is the convergence of the goals of these two ideologies that made knitting so attractive for the young, progressive women who fueled the urban knitting circle trend in the middle to late 1990s. So says Debbie Stoller, third-wave feminist, editor in chief of *BUST* magazine, and catalyst of the knitting circle proliferation throughout the United States, thanks to her first knitting book, *Stitch 'N Bitch: The Knitter's Handbook.*[2]

"Part of the new knitting revival, I really think, is reclaiming the domestic sphere," Stoller said in a February 2006 interview with this author. "Also, a lot of young people feel very manipulated by the larger corporate culture."[3]

Rather than let a prior generation of feminists define what are appropriate female activities, some new feminists choose to knit—as well as cook, sew, and engage in other domestic and craft skills. Likewise, some DIYers choose to knit their own clothes, make their own furniture, and, in general, supply some of their own needs and wants instead of purchasing items from large businesses that employ poorly paid workers in unhealthy work environments. To understand the motivations of the knitting avant-garde, it's best to take a closer look at DIY culture and modern feminism separately.

3

WHY DIY? THE DO-IT-YOURSELF MOVEMENT INSPIRES KNITTERS

The DIY movement is a reaction to the forces of technology, globalization, and stratification of socioeconomic groups. These aspects of modern life have sparked a desire among some people to reduce their consumption and rely less on the products of corporations. Another function of DIY culture is to allow adherents to have more intimate and organic relationships with others. DIYers say they connect more with friends, family, and charities by giving things made by their own hands. They also interact with like-minded people by organizing clubs that meet face-to-face and by communicating on the Internet, through DIY-themed Web sites, and, particularly, online journals called blogs.

Many young professionals are struggling to make their worlds more manageable. They are conscious of the exploitation of workers in developing nations, the hole in the ozone layer, and the diseases, birth defects, and allergies that seem to be coinciding with our rampant consumerism and its resultant waste. They are isolated by their long work hours and responsibilities, combined with family obligations. And they are inundated by demands and stimuli: colleagues can make requests at any hour thanks to voice mail and e-mail, and responses are expected quickly, especially from those equipped with personal digital assistants (PDAs). Television, Internet, radio, and even telemarketers bombard them with advertisements. And even so, this educated and privileged group enjoys the comforts and luxuries that relative affluence affords it.

The ethical and political concerns of this group somewhat resemble those of a prior generation of young people. The bohemians of the early twentieth century, also relatively privileged on the whole, opted to take a more radical stance against what they saw as America's wrongs. They congregated in New York City's Greenwich Village, where they took part in activism, open sexual relationships, politically charged salons, and the printing of leftist publications. They debated women's suffrage and reproductive rights, the need for labor laws, free love, and socialism. Their actions led to social change and great works of art and literature: Thomas Wolfe's novel, *Look Homeward, Angel*, the poems of Edna St. Vincent Millay, the plays of Eugene O'Neill and, later, the paintings of Jackson Pollock.

But many early liberals also sacrificed their marriages, their sanity, or their careers to their unattainable ideals. Jack Reed, a Harvard graduate who became devoted to socialism while writing for the radical monthly magazine, *The Masses*, even lost his life when he traveled to Russia on the eve of that nation's revolution.[1]

Today's socially conscious young elite is perhaps less idealistic and more cautious than the first American bohemians. They are more likely to make small changes to their own lifestyles rather than rally for revolution. Their actions are practical, like recycling, reusing, and making their own stuff rather than buying from Wal-Mart or The Gap.

They carve out patches of time and space to do pleasurable things and meet with like-minded people. They try to rein in their perfectly ordinary American urge to consume. They can exercise this bit of self-control in many different ways: by opting to refinish a piece of furniture rather than buy a new one, by making a CD mix of favorite songs as a wedding favor instead of spending hundreds of dollars on pointless knickknacks, or by knitting a sweater instead of buying one.

These kinds of activities, projects, and crafts comprise the DIY movement. DIY is going strong, as the success of publications such as *Make* and *Readymade* demonstrates.

In December 2005, the editors-in-chief of these DIY magazines were guests on National Public Radio (NPR)'s Talk of the Nation program. *Make* editor Mark Frauenfelder told NPR reporter Andrea Seabrook that, when the magazine launched, he had hoped for a circulation of about 10,000. As of the show's airdate, *Make's* circulation was higher than 100,000. Shoshana Berger, editor of *ReadyMade*, called the DIY audience a "sitting duck" for savvy marketers. The home-improvement magazine *This Old House* was more targeted to older and wealthier readers, she said. *Martha Stewart Living*, arguably the first major publication to revive domesticity and craft in the nineties, was "really about how to pick china," Berger said. "Nothing spoke to people in their twenties and thirties on a limited budget."[2]

Frauenfelder described *Make* as heir to the next generation of *Popular Mechanics* readers, with projects that tweak technology. Readers might learn to make a three-string guitar out of a cigar box or to rig a disposable camera to a kite to take aerial pictures.

ReadyMade projects focus on taking old or discarded objects and finding innovative ways to re-use them, and Berger described the readership as "pragmatic environmentalists." Through the magazine, readers can learn how to fashion a disco ball out of old compact disks (like the ones that Internet access providers send unsolicited in the mail.) Or, they might follow the advice of a past article titled "Pimp My Ikea," which urged readers to make something new and clever with random parts of the Swedish furniture giant's products. *ReadyMade's* median reader age is twenty-eight, though Berger claims the demography revolves around lifestyles and attitudes rather than age.

Why do readers of these magazines go to so much trouble when they could just buy something new? Berger argued that the current culture of mass production leaves many young people feeling cold. The DIY ethic springs from a desire to balk at that culture, she said. Frauenfelder concurred, noting the personal satisfaction that comes from creating and crafting. "When you make something, you have a part of yourself in it," he said. This is a sentiment heard repeatedly among knitters.

"I like creating things," said Bryna Subherwal, a twenty-nine-year-old knitter in New Haven, Connecticut. "I like being able to give things as gifts. It's somehow more personal when you put a lot of time into it. There's a nurturing aspect to it, too."[3]

Lauren Gorman, who owns the yarn shop Three Black Sheep in Northport, New York with her mother and a friend, said knitting gives her a satisfaction she couldn't get at her prior corporate job with a software company.[4]

"Almost all my work was done on the computer," Gorman said. "I never even worked with paper. Needlework brought me back to working with my hands. There's that sense of accomplishment that we don't get when everything is done for us. When I was knitting, I could say, 'I did this. I made this.'"

Many knitters interviewed for this book, particularly those with backgrounds in computer science, commented on the similarity between the most basic building blocks of computer programming and knitted fabric. Computer programming involves codes that use a binary system, that is, combinations of two digits: 0 and 1. All knitting derives from two fundamental stitches: knit and purl.

The relationship between high technology and textile craft is more than just theoretical. The Jacquard weaving loom, invented by Joseph Marie Jacquard in 1801, was the first machine to use punch card technology, an important development in the history of computer hardware. Each hole in the card corresponded to a hook holding threads on the loom, dictating whether that hook would move up or down and thus, controlling how threads were used to make a pattern in the fabric. The loom did no actual computing, but it was the direct inspiration for an early computer. In 1833, Charles Babbage used punch cards to program his difference engine, a mechanical calculator that tabulated polynomial functions.

It's no surprise, then, that people interested in computing might also enjoy using the same logic to create knitting stitch patterns.

Other knitters state deliberately that they knit to reduce their dependency on corporations for clothing.

"Among my friends, I think that it's a minor backlash against sweatshop labor—you know, if you make a sweater you don't have to buy one from J. Crew," said Jesse Loesberg of San Francisco, whose Web site, www.yarnboy.com, attests to a long history of male knitters. While he identified the DIY movement as a reason for knitting's popularity among his own social circle, he hesitated to attribute the trend to larger forces in general. "I think these things go in cycles," he said.[5]

On her Web site getcrafty.com, Jean Railla, a New York City mom in her thirties, says this about the craft movement: "It's about being both fashion-obsessed and simultaneously upset by sweat-shop labor practices."[6]

A sense of responsibility clearly motivates Cat Mazza, the founder of microRevolt (http://www.microRevolt.org/), a Web site and art collective devoted to raising awareness about sweatshops and globalization. The Web site states Mazza's goal this way: "microRevolt projects investigate the dawn of sweatshops in early industrial capitalism to inform the current crisis of global expansion and the feminization of labor."[7]

A highlight of the Web site is knitPro, a web application that can translate digital images into knit, crochet, needlepoint, and cross-stitch patterns. The application essentially allows knitters and other needle-crafters to swipe any brand logo or design simply by uploading a digital photo of the image. The Web site shows knitted garments that incorporate and play with well-known corporate images and logos, like Mickey Mouse's ears and Nike's swoosh.

Mazza said creating knitPro was easy because one pixel equals one stitch. She quickly recognized that, because knitPro is so useful, it would create an audience for the issues she addresses on microRevolt. Furthermore, she believes knitters are in a rare position to understand the plight of textile workers.

"Contemporary knitters understand the labor process that goes into making a garment," Mazza said. "It takes a lot of energy, time, and frustration, but it's also a lot of fun. I thought this would be an empathetic audience to people making consumer goods."[8]

Critics of logo knitting have argued that using corporate images in handmade items could inadvertently promote the brands they represent. Mazza explained her rationale for using corporate logos and images in hand-knit items.

"It's really in the tradition of art-making," she said. "Some art deals with making a pretty picture, trying to recreate a beautiful scene. Other art, and the kind I align microRevolt more with, is social commentary."

The use of corporate logos and trademarks is, "ironic commentary art practice," she said. Beyond that, a long tradition exists in the history of textiles of embedding images into fabric that reflect some significant aspect of the maker or wearer's life or surroundings. For instance, in Peru, a knitted hat might bear the image of an indigenous animal that lives in the maker's environment and is important to his everyday life, Mazza said. Fair Isle designs knitted in the north of Scotland often use colors and shapes that have cultural significance.

"I was interested in that sort of tradition," Mazza said. Things like Nike's swoosh and Mickey Mouse's ears were the same kind of symbols in her own environment, she said, "as somebody who lives in late capitalism and, at the time, lived in New York City, where you are always bombarded with logos and symbols of corporate power."

Incorporating trademarked logos and images is also a form of activism, since it commits a violation of the trademark, Mazza said. "It gets people to think about what the symbol means."

Mazza rejects the argument that people, particularly children, might not understand the irony she intends to reflect by using corporate images in her knitted garments.

"I don't think we should eliminate children as an audience for critique of the media and education about sweatshop labor," Mazza said. She believes people underestimate children's ability to understand such commentary, and she also thinks children deserve to know about sweatshop conditions, "because children are often employed in sweatshops."

Mazza was an art student at Carnegie Mellon University (CMU) when she first started thinking about the relationships between art, technology, textiles, and women's work, she said. CMU curriculums place a strong emphasis on technology, and it was there that she began working with new media in her art. After college, she was a founding member of Eyebeam, a New York City-based organization that explores the intersection of art and science through education, research, supplying artistic resources, and hosting exhibitions. Working with technology became Mazza's daily grind, and she craved a more organic and tactile activity. In 1999, she asked her grandmother to teach her how to knit for a second time, she said. She vaguely recalled that in her young childhood, her grandmother gave her a knitting lesson.

Mazza developed the idea for microRevolt while working on an M.F.A. at Rensselaer Polytechnic Institute in Troy, New York. She had learned about exploitation of textile workers through an anti-sweatshop nonprofit organization in Maine called Peace Through Inter-American

Community Action (PICA). She also discovered that America's Northeast, where she lived, was the birthplace of textile factories and of women's protests against unfair work conditions.

Mazza says her aim with microRevolt is not to garner the attention of executives at large clothing companies. "I think it would be optimistic to think these corporations would identify what microRevolt is doing as any kind of threat," Mazza said. "To me, that's totally absurd."

Young knitters who embed their hand knits with corporate logos could never generate enough garments to affect the markets of corporations, she said. Mazza hoped that, by violating their trademarks, she might start a dialogue with corporate giants known for outsourcing to sweatshops, but so far not a single one has contacted her, she said.

The goal of microRevolt has to be smaller—to engage contemporary knitters, who she says have a tacit knowledge of garment making. By a tacit knowledge, Mazza means one that cannot easily be explained, only conveyed through shared experience. Learning to ride a bicycle is also most often done tacitly. "For me, I learned (knitting) best when my grandmother was over the shoulder showing me," Mazza said, and that is how most knitters learn the skill. Mazza says this "indescribable and meaningful," understanding and connection among makers is something that scholars on labor studies use to describe factory work.

Mazza has not given up on getting the attention of large corporations. She continues to collect squares for the Nike blanket project, a work in progress that is nonetheless being exhibited at galleries and other sites around the world. The blanket, fourteen feet wide and five feet high, fuses together knitted and crocheted squares that display Nike trademarked material. The squares continue to be made and donated to the project from knitters and crocheters around the globe who oppose sweatshop labor practices.

Mazza said she gets a lot of feedback that the blanket should travel for as long as possible to serve as an education piece and accumulate more squares. The artist launched the project hoping to give the completed blanket to Phil Knight, Nike's chairman of the board of directors. Mazza said she still hopes to give the blanket to Knight eventually.

The microRevolt Web site also provides some straightforward education, like describing a landmark tragedy that spurred labor law reform in America. This was the Triangle Waist Factory fire in New York City on March 25, 1911, which killed 146 workers—all but twenty-three of them women and girls.

David Von Drehle's book, *Triangle: The Fire that Changed America*, gives a gripping account of this fire at what was then New York's largest manufacturer of women's blouses. The blaze broke out when a match or cigarette butt ignited a bin of fabric beneath a shirt cutter's table. Within about five minutes, flames filled the entire eighth floor of the skyscraper off lower Manhattan's Washington Square. Within fifteen minutes, fire spread to the building's ninth and tenth floors, which also housed Triangle factory and office space. About fifty workers were trapped in the factory because some doors were locked and all opened inward, a design fault that effectively blocked the exits as people charged forward to flee. And yet, not all the deaths were caused by burning or smoke inhalation. Many trapped victims jumped from the building's windows, and others fell through the windows as fire and panicked fellow workers encroached upon them. A reporter on the scene, William Gunn Shepard, wrote that he saw fifty-four bodies piled on the sidewalks. About two-dozen people died when the faulty fire escape they were trapped upon collapsed.

Like most garment factories in New York at the time, the Triangle had no firewalls, fire doors, fire stairs, or automatic sprinklers. The horrific spectacle of the blaze shocked New Yorkers and called attention to the need for greater fire safety measures. In 1913, as a result of public outcry over the Triangle fire, the New York State legislature enacted sweeping and unprecedented commercial fire safety laws and labor reform.

Safety flaws that plagued the Asch Building, which housed the Triangle Waist Factory, were addressed. Sprinklers were required in skyscrapers, and doors had to swing outward and remain unlocked. Fire drills were mandated in larger factories.

Laws were also enacted to protect women and children in the workplace. Sweatshops, the small factories that entrepreneurial immigrants used to set up in their tenement homes at the turn of the twentieth century, were deemed illegal.[9]

The name microRevolt is an abbreviation of a concept called "molecular revolutions" originated by French philosopher, Felix Guattari. Guattari supported the idea that small acts of resistance, rather than major movements, can result in social change. Mazza said she views knitting itself, making things by hand, as a small act of resistance against the larger consumer culture.

One can argue that simply knitting can serve as an act of resistance because it reduces the need for store-bought clothing from unknown sources. Few people have the time or inclination to make all their own clothes, as the American colonists did on the eve of their revolution from Britain. And yet, a person who makes some of her own clothes can know that what she wears is the product of her own hands, of work that she enjoyed. She probably spent money on yarn, and no one can deny that the coveting of lush fibers is flagrant participation in capitalist indulgence. But it's far more likely that the yarn was produced by a small company, perhaps even by a farm family, or a housebound mother who dyes and spins fleece while her infant naps.

Take, for instance, Katie Franceschi, a mother of twin toddlers who sells her hand-dyed yarn, patterns, and hand-knitted garments on her Web site, www.bungalowbuns.com.[10] She even sells soakers, those knitted infants' pants with string-gathered waists and legs, which women laboriously produced during World War II when a rubber shortage made elastic scarce.

Franceschi said she took up knitting as an adult out of pure necessity. Her mother taught her to knit when she was seven, but it didn't stick. She just didn't like it that much. In fact, she took up quilting for professional reasons before she resorted to knitting.

She was college educated, married, and living in Des Moines, Iowa, where she worked as an office manager for a sewing machine sales company. Customers there wanted to see examples of quilting done on the machines, so Franceschi took up that craft and turned it into a business.

Then, at twenty-two, Franceschi learned she was pregnant with twins. Quilting with her cumbersome, long-arm sewing machine became impossible at a certain point in her pregnancy.

To make ends meet, she got a sales job in a department store, but she remained concerned about family finances. Just paying for twins' paper diapers could become a major expense. She looked into using cloth diapers and, online, she learned about the revival of soakers, a bygone baby garment that was popular in the forties.

"Wool is so absorbent that it can retain thirty percent of its weight in water before it feels wet," Franceschi told me. "It also has antimicrobial properties that reduce the need for washing to about once every three weeks."

Once soiled, soakers can be washed and then re-used. And yet, even soakers might put a dent in a tight budget. They cost about $30 each, and Franceschi estimated that she would need at least fifteen.

"That's why I started knitting again," she said. "I kind of had that nesting thing going on. I think I probably knit twenty soakers in six months."

Franceschi got good at knitting soakers and so, www.bungalowbuns. com was born. When customers started asking for soakers in pretty colors, Franceschi realized the cost of colored yarns would consume more of her already narrow profit margin. She decided to learn how to dye yarn herself. Soon, she saw that her hand-dyed yarns addressed a larger market than the niche for soakers. She turned the bulk of her online moneymaking efforts toward hand-dyes. She also plans to start a new Web site with two other hand-dyers: one in Maryland and, the other, in Montana.

Franceschi said she kept knitting for her own enjoyment after giving up most of the soaker business. She moved on to more advanced projects, like knitting lace. Though she usually knits alone, she said her community of online friends provides a special kind of inspiration. She thinks the Internet may be partially responsible for the current knitting renaissance. I learned about Franceschi through the Internet; I saw her pattern for a baby's pacifier cord in *Knitty*, the online knitting magazine.

Another woman who turned knitting into a career is Lynn Wilson of Trumbull, Connecticut.[11] Wilson said she was a teenager when her best friend's mother taught her to knit. That was in the seventies, and Wilson said she lost interest in the craft quickly. "At the time I thought, 'This is boring. This is not cool,'" she said.

Later in her life, her sister-in-law reintroduced her to knitting, and Wilson became so enthralled with the skill that she even started teaching knitting classes at a local yarn shop, Knitting Central in Fairfield, Connecticut.

Wilson started designing patterns as a way to present appropriate projects in her classes. These early creations were things like baby clothes and hats. She found that students enjoyed her designs and would often ask for copies of her patterns. Wilson became known for her felting projects, but she wanted to broaden her appeal. She began designing a wider range of items. Before long, several yarn companies approached Wilson asking her to invent garments for them.

In 2005, Wilson, who is in her early fifties, took a big leap of faith. She quit her full-time job as a development editor for art at a book publishing company, and she launched her own business, Lynn Wilson Designs.

"The knitting just took off," Wilson said. In her career as an editor, she always thought she was pretty creative. Her new work is more creative, still, she says. "The ideas come so fast," Wilson said. "I need forty-five hours a week to knit everything that's in my head."

Wilson said she barely feels in control of the professional journey she is taking. "I kind of feel I've been put on this path," she said. "Things are happening through not a lot of my effort. I'm riding in this car down the road, and I'm not steering."

Reflecting on why knitting is such a force in her life now but didn't draw her as a teen, Wilson repeated a sentiment expressed by many knitters of her era. "Women started to go back to work and didn't want to knit during their free time," which was rare, she said.

The tradition among women of passing knitting skills from mother to daughter skipped her generation, so her age group got interested later in life, she said. Wilson said she thoroughly understands why young women today find knitting so appealing.

"It's great to be able to knit," she said. "It's portable. You can pick it up and put it down. It's social and practical. I think one difference between knitting and other crafts is that it's making something useful. How many needlepointed pillow covers can you make? I think we have so much stress in our lives and so little free time, if we're going to give up free time for a hobby, we want tangible results."

The portability of knitting also makes it possible for professionals and all kinds of busy people to fit it into their lifestyles, Wilson said. "I know a couple of people who are into scrapbooking, but again, you need space for that," Wilson said. One needs hardly any time, space, or concentration to knit, she said. She even knits behind the wheel of her car when traffic is at a standstill on the often-congested Merritt Parkway in Connecticut. She keeps sock projects in the back seat, at the ready.

Another draw to knitting is the quality and variety of yarns available today, she said. "In a shop sometimes you'll feel a certain karma, or a skein of yarn will speak to you," Wilson said. "That had a lot to do with me going down this path."

Wilson said she enjoys how women from all kinds of socioeconomic backgrounds find themselves bonding in her knitting classes. By the third session of any given class, she said, she witnesses a chemistry developing among her students.

She also appreciates the respect she gets from young women taking up the craft. "If you're a young business woman coming to a knitting class, you're not there for the power trip," she said. "You're there to find common ground with people. A lot of people take classes for the camaraderie. A lot of people develop friendships."

Wilson has also started a local chapter of The Knitting Guild of America (TGKA), called the Soundview Knitting Guild. Members meet in Trumbull once a month to socialize and share knowledge. The guild also sponsors special events such as trunk shows, retreats, visits from masseuses, and fashion shows.

Stories abound of women who have used knitting to change their workaday lives into professions that let them follow their bliss. In 2004 in Northport, New York, three generations of women turned a daydream into a reality when they opened a yarn shop together.[12]

Like the other women interviewed in this section, Lauren Gorman revisited knitting in recent years after a long hiatus. In 2003, Gorman went with her mother, Linda Thury, and her close friend, Kathy Redman, to a knitting camp. In their travels they visited a large, fabulous knitting store that captured their imaginations. Driving home to Northport, the three women gushed over the store and daydreamed about owning a yarn shop, Gorman said.

"I thought, 'How can I do this every day, make it not be a hobby, and sort of legitimize myself a little bit?'" Gorman said.

Soon thereafter, Gorman said she was buying a birthday present for one of Redman's kids at a toy store on Northport's Main Street. The space next door had just gone up for rent. The narrow room previously housed a Victorian gift shop and was painted darkly with purple and pink walls and a black floor. As dark as it appeared when empty, the place spoke to her, she said.

At the birthday party, Gorman mentioned the available retail spot to Redman. "It was like kismet," Gorman said. "Everybody at the party was talking about real estate. Gorman said she never had to tell Redman what her intentions were for the space. "A yarn shop?" Redman asked.

After the party, Gorman stayed behind at Redman's house. The two mothers brainstormed in the backyard. "It was one of those perfect summer days and we started talking for hours and taking notes," Gorman said.

Neither woman had ever owned a business, though Gorman had worked in a yarn shop and knew something of how they operated. When Gorman called her mother to ask her to join their business partnership, she answered immediately, "I'm in."

Before the week was up, the women had agreed to rent the Main Street storefront. They made lots of changes, painting the store a light honey color and searching the giant Swedish furniture store, Ikea, for fixtures like cubbyhole shelving for displaying yarn. Lauren's husband, a plumber, installed a bathroom, and other family members helped out with electrical work. In a year, they were ready to open their shop, Three Black Sheep. In the two years since they started their business, Gorman said, some of their own customers and employees have launched their own yarn shops.

A few years back, it was tough to find a good local yarn store. Today they abound, and many are thriving. I asked Lauren why she thinks knitting has caught on recently. "I think part of it has to do with the fact that we've become so global as a society," Gorman said. "Nobody makes anything, or does anything or talks to anybody."

People's desire to make crafts is a backlash against the fact that making things is no longer essential, she said. "We've lost a lot of that sense of home and the basics," Gorman said. "People don't even cook anymore. Our lives have become so much easier, but we don't have contact." Gorman said that her customers counteract a lack of intimacy by knitting together in the cozy space of her shop.

"(At the store) we've watched friendships develop between people who take classes together," Gorman said. "We have this community that didn't exist before. These are women who lived in the same community for years and never knew each other, because their kids are different ages. Knitting just seems to be trans-generational."

"We solve all the world's problems at some of our knit-ins," Gorman joked. "People are looking for that connection. We're connected in so many ways, but we're also disconnected."

Gorman was in college when she first took up knitting. She was experiencing chronic pain, and her doctor told her to get a hobby. She chose knitting because she likes sweaters, she said. Over the years she got interested in other needlework, particularly embroidery.

"After I had my son, it was hard to have needles and scissors around," she said. "And by the time I had time to sit, someone needed something," she said. Around that time, about nine years ago, the local chapter of the Embroiderers' Guild of America sponsored a community service project in which members knitted hats for prematurely born babies. Gorman decided to knit a hat. Since then, she says, only about ten days have passed when she hasn't knitted. Her kids are still in school. She lives two blocks from her shop on Main Street, and the business is doing well.

Gorman attributes the popularity of knitting to the way the hobby can fit into a busy life. Knitting is portable, and it can be done in short spurts, making use of spare moments found waiting in line and riding on buses, trains, and subways.

"I think it's also the fibers out there," Gorman said. "You don't have to be really great at knitting to make something really great." Projects are often simple enough to be done while talking or participating with a group. "I can do it with my kids around," she said. "I don't have to have a special place to do it."

Aware that knitting is enjoying a heyday right now, Gorman and her partners thought hard about how to make their business sustainable, she said. "We never really set ourselves up as a trendy shop," she said, referring to yarn stores that sell lots of novelty yarns. Yarn representatives refer to these as scarf shops, because their clientele may not yet be interested in doing more than rudimentary knitting, such as making scarves.

"We had that traffic," Gorman said. "But I think a lot of the people who started off saying, 'I just want to knit scarves,' are getting into full-fledged sweater knitting."

Gorman hopes to encourage that trend. The shop, like many others, offers classes at least once a week and a free knitting clinic, where customers can consult with an in-house knitting expert on projects that present them with problems. Education is part of their strategy to keep people interested in knitting.

"You have to offer them something," Gorman said. She tries to provide classes at Three Black Sheep at a variety of times and to respond to customers' requests to learn particular techniques.

The knitting boom in the United States is also creating economic opportunities for women in other parts of the Americas. Rural women in Uruguay gain regular work and a social outlet through Manos del Uruguay, a collective of small cooperatives. The company makes a soft, lumpy, one-ply yarn dyed in a range of supersaturated colors. Manos del Uruguay claims to employ 400 artisans at seventeen cooperatives, as well as 120 independent artisans and 50 other technicians and administrative employees, paying them fair wages. Work at the collective also provides a social outlet for these women who might otherwise be relatively isolated, living on farms.

This brings us to another motivation behind the DIY movement: the desire for more meaningful communication and social interaction. Cell phones, computers, and PDAs like Palms and Blackberries keep us connected to family, friends, and work at nearly every moment. And yet often, these devices transmit brief communications, lacking in intimacy. Often, they are messages that relay demands. Sometimes, as in the case of most SPAM e-mails or calls from telemarketers, the messages are wholly unwelcome and intrusive. In spite of the many messages we field every day, many people feel isolated and crave greater intimacy.

Knitters are using their craft to carve out personal space and to revive real, face-to-face interactions. Some do it through knitting circles and related organizations. Others make their communities online. As we will explore in Chapter 8, Knitting into the Ether, the communications of bloggers and participants in web rings use language that is so specific to the knitting subculture that it actually helps knitters to find each other on the Internet.

4

IT'S A GIRL THING: FEMINISM AND DOMESTICITY CONVERGE

Among the new knitters and crafters are many women who consider themselves feminists. Enjoying crafts and domestic skills like cooking, decorating, and even cleaning required these modern women to think hard about how these traditionally feminine interests might be reconciled with a feminist identity.

In the sixties and seventies, feminism's second wave disparaged domesticity and the skills that went along with it. Knitting, sewing, cooking, and cleaning were responsibilities that tied the woman to the home and prevented her from doing what was deemed more meaningful work, that is, work that gave access to money and power in the largely male spheres of business and politics.

In *The Feminine Mystique,* Betty Friedan blamed homemaking and the exclusively domestic lifestyle of many American women for what she called, "the problem that has no name."[1] By the late fifties, Friedan said, the average age at which women married had dropped to twenty, and it was descending into the teens. Meanwhile, the proportion of women on college campuses was shrinking, from 47 percent in 1920 to 35 percent in 1958. The media was selling the notion that a woman's sole route to happiness was the pursuit of marriage and motherhood.

Friedan believed that women were not content to be only housewives. They needed something more to fulfill them, and that something was education and a career. Her message rang true for countless American women in the seventies and eighties.

So it happened that the children of Friedan's generation of feminists—today's young women—came to view domestic skills and crafts in general as somewhat backward and embarrassing. The feminist who actually enjoyed one of these activities would have to hide her shameful habit from her progressive friends.

Jean Railla, a New York City wife and mom in her thirties who publishes the Web magazine getcrafty.com, describes the prevailing attitude toward domestic skills this way:[2]

> From cooking to cleaning to caring for children, our culture views "women's work" as stupid, simple, suffocating—things that can easily be replaced by mechanization, crappy fast food, hiring poor women and neglect—precisely because women have always done them.

Railla notes that even feminists look down upon women's work because they have internalized patriarchal thinking. Somewhere in the middle to late nineties, many modern women decided to reconsider domesticity, femininity, and the work and leisure roles that women have historically occupied. I believe that the female role models women saw in the media during the prior decade motivated this change of heart.

During the eighties and nineties, America watched two women rise to power, fame, and wealth on par with the most successful men: Oprah Winfrey and Martha Stewart. Both of these women exerted a tremendous hold on the public imagination, and particularly on how women viewed the scope of possibilities for success in their lives. Interestingly, perhaps even ironically, Winfrey and Stewart achieved greatness by male standards while they encouraged women to embrace activities that have typically fallen into the female realm.

Winfrey's daytime television show popularized book clubs. Young professional women started gathering in cafes and each other's homes after work to talk about novels. Though the literati sometimes expressed contempt for Oprah's Book Club picks—*The Corrections* author Jonathan Franzen infamously scoffed at his novel's inclusion on her reading list—Winfrey's focus on books arguably saved the fiction publishing industry. Just a few years before Oprah's Book Club made its debut in 1996, the market for novels was in a serious rut. The Lannan Foundation, which funds projects supporting top artists, writers, and activists for native populations, in the early nineties sponsored a novelists' panel discussion entitled, "The Life of the Novel, the Death of the Novel." The discussion, which I witnessed at New York City's Town Hall, allowed American authors such as Norman Mailer, Paule Marshall, Oscar Hijuelos, and Mona Simpson to publicly ponder the fate of the genre. Mailer commented that, unlike in prior generations, it was rare in the early nineties for people to be able to discuss a novel with friends. So few people were reading novels, and even those who did rarely read the same novels as their friends and colleagues. Winfrey's espousal of reading changed this. It also persuaded many young professional women to think deliberately about setting aside time for leisure and society, and this helped set the stage for other changes in their busy lives.

The rise to prominence of Martha Stewart also marked a change in the overall attitude toward domestic arts. By 1993, when Stewart launched the half-hour television show *Martha Stewart Living* to complement her magazine of the same title, hers was literally a household name. For a certain segment of the female, affluent population, Stewart was a godsend. She taught the wives of corporate executives how to be great hostesses and how to decorate a home tastefully, and she taught many more women how to dream of domestic bliss. Eventually, her distinctive style, the magazine's great photography, and Stewart's business acumen—questionable stock sales excepted—broadened her audience to include much of the nation.

Still, younger professional women sought their own heroine. Many of those who educated themselves and worked hard to succeed in traditional male careers remained wary of Martha Stewart's message. For one thing, her projects were typically elaborate and somewhat costly, and her aesthetic, though attractive, was clearly that of an upper-middle class woman, thoroughly comfortable with her social and economic status. A significant portion of young urban and suburban, college-educated women didn't view themselves as part of Stewart's target audience.

A new "problem that has no name" emerged for many women in Generations X and Y, in their teens, twenties, and thirties during the nineties. Again, the problem was a discrepancy between the female identity crafted by a prior generation and the identity these women wished to create for themselves.

Enter, Debbie Stoller. Stoller is a New Yorker with a Ph.D. in the psychology of women from Yale University and editor of *BUST*, a glossy, celebrity-filled feminist magazine. But knitting is what made her truly famous. Her name is well known among young urban knitters because she put them on the map with the 2003 publication of her first knitting how-to book, *Stitch 'N Bitch: The Knitter's Handbook*.

In *Stitch 'N Bitch*, Stoller described her struggle to resolve her beloved knitting heritage with her feminist legacy. She comes from a long line of Dutch knitters, women who knitted out of necessity and didn't consider their handiwork to be creative or artful. Stoller's book recounts how rations in World War II required her grandmother to improvise knitted underwear for her children by unraveling a bedspread Stoller's great-grandmother had knitted a generation before.

Stoller didn't embrace knitting until adulthood. She described in *Stitch 'N Bitch* how she struggled with knitting as a child and gave it up, influenced in part by the messages of the seventies' women's rights movement. Feminists of that era taught her that women were meant for greater things than keeping house.

Then, during a year spent living in Holland, Stoller found herself intrigued by a roommate's knitting and asked her grandmother to re-introduce her to the craft. She picked up the sticks in 1999, despite her adherence to feminism.

She also began to question why knitting was greeted with such dis-dain, and the answer, it seemed to her, was ironically misogynistic:

> It seemed to me that the main difference between knitting and, say, fish-ing or woodworking or basketball, was that knitting had traditionally been done by women. As far as I could tell that was the only reason it had gotten such a bad rap. And that's when it dawned on me: All those people who looked down on knitting—and housework, and housewives—were not being feminist at all. In fact, they were being anti-feminist, since they seemed to think that only those things that men did, or had done, were worthwhile. Sure, feminism had changed the world, and young girls all across the country had formed soccer leagues, and were grow-ing up to become doctors and astronauts and senators. But why weren't boys learning to knit and sew? Why couldn't we all—women and men alike—take the same kind of pride in the work our mothers had always done as we did in the work of our fathers?[3]

Stoller decided that she would fight to improve knitting's image. She launched New York City's first Stitch 'N Bitch group. She knitted in public and raved about the joys of knitting. She published articles about knitting in *BUST*.

Stoller came to believe that second generation feminists, Friedan and her contemporaries, eschewed knitting because they thought it subjugated women by restraining them to a role of service to others. What they failed to understand was that knitting, even when done for others, benefited the knitter, as well.

When Stoller whipped out her knitting projects on the New York City subway, she noted the reactions of fellow riders. Older women gave her knowing looks. She presumed they understood the pleasures of knitting.

"I always like to say it's delicious, it's nice and calming and soothing, in the same way that playing Tetris is," Stoller told me. "There are so many things that I enjoy about it, the sensuousness of working with yarn and needles, the comforting, rhythmic quality, the sense of learn-ing something new as an adult."

When Stoller knitted in public, young men and women, as well as women of her mother's generation, were more apt to stare in shock. "I might as well have been churning butter on the cross-town bus," she wrote in her first knitting book.

But she noticed that other young women were knitting in public, too. Knitting made its comeback in the middle to late nineties, when some stylish new knitting books were published. And yet, Stoller never thought the trend would endure quite so long.

"When I first started knitting in 1999, yarn stores were still shutting down all over the place," she said. She confessed, she thought she had missed the boat. "I was really surprised when it was as popular as it was," Stoller said. "I don't think I would've predicted that knitting would be this popular."

In fact, her efforts may have turned the knitting "boat" into a mammoth cruise liner; she furthers the knitting cause these days by leading knitting-themed travels, including, in 2007, a cruise to Mexico. *Stitch 'N Bitch* was a huge success. Stoller's heartfelt and informed testimony to the value and joy of knitting turned on a generation of young American adults to the craft.

Part of the book's appeal was that it featured projects that acknowledged a younger woman's lifestyle. Funky patterns included an iPod cozy, a cat bed that makes clever use of trendy eyelash yarn, and a sweater with skulls on the elbows. *Publisher's Weekly* said, "this slightly offensive, sassy guide—which could easily have been subtitled 'The Bad Girls' Guide to Knitting' will undoubtedly appeal to this new generation of knitters." And it did.

In 2004, Stoller's second knitting book *Stitch 'N Bitch Nation*, introduced even more playful patterns: a yoga mat, fuzzy monster slippers, and cell phone covers that look like kittens and pigs. The cheesy, sexist silhouette of a nude girl that sometimes decorates truck mud flaps was emblazoned on the front of a black, knitted tank top. And a knitted doll version of punk rock icon Joey Ramone garnered plenty of press attention.

As this book was being written, Stoller's *Stitch 'N Bitch* titles included more than 560,000 books in print according to her publisher, Workman Publishing Company. And that was before the release of Stoller's third how-to book on yarn crafts, *Stitch 'N Bitch Crochet: The Happy Hooker.*

Stoller says her big push on behalf of knitting was inspired by a broader effort among the latest generation of feminists, dubbed the third wave. These feminists embrace traditionally female activities like crafting and homemaking and behaviors deemed feminine by the larger culture, such as wearing dresses and makeup. When interviewed for this book, Stoller credited third-wave feminists, rather than just herself, with jump-starting the knitting craze.

"There's a couple of different things I think led to (knitting) becoming so popular," Stoller said. "For me, the important one is that a couple of feminists were thinking about aspects of women's culture that were rejected by previous generations of feminists as out-and-out oppressive.

Girly-girl things, forms of display, domesticity, were they oppressive in and of themselves?"

Young women who choose to be stay-at-home mothers, to wear sexy clothing, or to craft, for instance, don't necessarily reject feminism. Stoller demonstrated her advocacy of that viewpoint during a publicity interview for Powell's Books, where she named two supersexualized pop idols as her inspiration: Madonna and Courtney Love. The third woman in her triumvirate of female power muses was another kind of celebrity: Martha Stewart.

Not all modern-day feminists embrace these ideals of the third wave. Not even every knitting feminist accepts these notions. The person who drove this point home to me is the biggest knitting blog celebrity in the Western knitting world, Stephanie Pearl-McPhee, also known as the Yarn Harlot. Pearl-McPhee, who knew I had interviewed Stoller previously, mentioned that she and Stoller share the same publisher and that they have chatted before at events.

"One day I'm going to get drunk at a cocktail party and ask her what the mud flap girl tank top is all about," Pearl-McPhee said. "I know she's a more serious feminist and everything, and that she's got a degree from Yale, but I don't get the mud flap girl."[4]

Pearl-McPhee got pretty riled up. As a mother of three girls and Stoller's contemporary, she said, she felt confused that they had interpreted the message of the seventies' feminists so differently.

"For me, the larger issues around feminism were always about women having the right to choose, men not owning most of the property in the world, and women not being exploited as cheap labor," Pearl-McPhee said. "Embracing your inner girly-girl, I think that's already been accepted by a lot of women. I'm a 38-year-old woman with unshaved legs, and I'm trying to figure out what's up with the mud flap girl. I'd love to sit down and figure that out."

One could argue that the mud flap girl image, when hijacked on a tank top in Stoller's second knitting book, is displayed ironically, and that by wearing it, a feminist claims the image as her own and diffuses its power to degrade her. Pearl-McPhee heard me out on this argument and rejected it.

"I don't buy the whole, 'taking it back,' thing," Pearl-McPhee said. She doesn't believe African Americans do themselves a service by using derogatory terms against themselves, either, she said.

Pearl-McPhee, known widely as a humorist, was dead serious about this issue. She says she and Stoller are in opposite camps regarding knitting and feminism. "She says knitting is a feminist privilege," Pearl-McPhee said. "I think it's a feminist reward."

"I think it's absolutely no coincidence that my mother doesn't knit," said Pearl-McPhee. Very few young women knitted, at least in public, during the seventies and eighties, she noted.

"I think it's almost that they couldn't afford to," Pearl-McPhee said. "In order to break down notions of what women were capable of, they could not be seen engaging in traditionally female activities at all. Learning how to be a doctor is hard enough. They're having a hard enough time accepting you're there." Young women today should be grateful to their mothers' generation of feminists, Pearl-McPhee said.

"I think women our age owe them a great deal," she said. "Though feminism still has a long way to go, it is possible for someone to knit in law school and still become a lawyer. They were busy expanding the idea of what women were capable of. Society learns too slowly."

She added that the issues second-wave feminists addressed are still relevant. She recounted a story of how she learned about gender inequity first-hand in one of her early jobs after graduating from art school.

Pearl-McPhee was working as a photographer for a Canadian studio when she became pregnant. She was assigned to train the male photographer who would replace her during her yearlong maternity leave. At some point during the training, her male trainee asked her to explain something he saw on his pay stub. That was when she realized the studio was already paying him more than they paid her, though she had been working there for three years.

After she cried foul to a Canadian agency that addresses such issues, her employer insisted the pay discrepancy was not sexist. It was the product of necessity, the boss said. Men could not be hired for such a low wage. They would not accept it, she was told.

Pearl-McPhee noted that maternity leave was computed based on one's wages, minus 15 percent, the estimate of the employee's typical costs for working—transportation, parking, and meals, for example. Pearl-McPhee's protest was enough to get her employer to adjust her maternity leave to be based on what the male employee was making. She could have fought for back pay, she said, but that would have required litigation at her own expense.

Pearl-McPhee is one of many knitting women who continue to align themselves more with the second wave of feminists. Some of these women might not find humor or liberation in the third wave's reclamation of the mud flap girl image. Upon learning that image was under fire, Stoller had this to say: "I've devoted the last thirty years of my life to studying feminism and trying to draw conclusions about which strategies might be the most successful for creating a more egalitarian society for women and men. (Yup, I was a second-wave feminist at fourteen!)" Stoller said. "I've also been financially independent since the age of seventeen, paid my way through college, was on scholarship in grad school, and have been working full-time ever since, usually more than one job at a time, so believe me, I understand the plight of the working woman. But I think the queer rights movement (and the riot grrrls of the 1990s) were onto something really important when they hit on the strategy of 'reclaiming' as a useful means of effecting change in the culture. I've used a similar strategy in *BUST* magazine and in my efforts to help make knitting be seen as a positive rather than negative activity for women (and men) to engage in. I know that feminist irony isn't for everyone, but context is everything when it comes to cultural meanings. As far as I see it, a woman meticulously knitting a mudflap girl into a tank top completely changes the meaning of that figure, sort of elevating the image of a woman's body as a thing used by truckers to protect their wheels from mud, to an image that can be worn with pride (and a wink) by young knitters. There isn't anything wrong with the image itself. After all, it's just a woman's figure. It's the way it's been used (on mudflaps) that's given it its negative connotations. But if we use it in a different way, we have the opportunity to give it a different meaning. That goes for mudflap girls, and it goes for knitting, too."

Meanwhile, in the *Guardian*, a magazine published in the United Kingdom, writer Zoe Williams stood up for Stoller's brand of feminism. Media outlets may report that women are disenchanted by feminism, that the workplace has not brought women the satisfaction that they thought it possessed. Williams discusses how Stoller turns the tables on that antifeminist argument.

"There are far too few people like Stoller, pointing out the obvious—some women find work a grind because that's exactly what it is. Men find it a grind as well," Williams wrote.[5] Women should be as free as men to roam between various activities without worrying about whether they are feminine or not, Williams proposed. Whether those activities are ultimately gratifying is beside the point.

"There is a stigma to knitting that is completely there because it's something women always did," Stoller told me. "Now women have been encouraged to do male activities. Little girls ended up playing soccer. I also need to see little boys knitting, otherwise we're still really valuing men's activities more than women's."

Stoller's dream appears to be coming true. The political climate now allows some men, those who are brave enough to accept stereotyping, to knit in public, just as men did in Central Park during war-driven knit-ins. A few Web sites devoted to male knitters have popped up on the Internet in recent years. Blogs by male knitters abound.

At Battell Chapel, Yale University's Christian worship space in New Haven, Connecticut, Sachin Shivaram stuck out in a mostly female knitting circle. Shivaram, a former management consultant and current Yale Law School student, was the picture of conservatism in his pressed blue oxford shirt and khakis. He quietly plied his needles, knitting for charity along with other congregation members.

"I saw the sign-up at the gym," he said. "I always wanted to learn. My grandmother knits. I love it. Sometimes I go home after studying and knit, listen to the radio and have a beer."[6]

Shivaram said he finds the craft relaxing and almost mindless. He likes working with his hands and enjoys being able to socialize while he knits, he said. He claimed no knowledge of a knitting trend among young people.

A fellow knitter, Kathy Lindbeck, said her brother asked her to teach him to knit.[7] He has been enjoying a hobby of tying flies for fishing and realized he likes the tactile nature of that hobby. "He wants to find something else he can do to occupy his hands," Lindbeck said. "He was a chain smoker for fifty-six years."

The greater prevalence of men knitting in public pleases Stoller. "I'm really very happy to see it," Stoller said. "It does mean that the stigma is beginning to disintegrate. What's really cool is that little kids are knitting."

In Philadelphia, a schoolteacher teaches her elementary students to knit. A number of how-to knitting books are being published specifically for children. The sewing machine company Singer is marketing a plastic machine, packaged in pink and purple, that automatically knits tubes of various sizes. You can find this knitting machine sold among toys, not just craft supplies. Though interest in knitting skipped at least one generation of mothers, it is making a comeback among young children and teens.

"They have no idea that it's gendered," Stoller said of the little boys and girls who are taking up the craft. "They're too young to have grandmothers who knit. Their grandmothers had rejected knitting already."

Even several adult knitters who were interviewed for this book claimed that their grandmothers could not teach them to knit. One of them was Zabet Stewart, a web designer and cofounder of the Gothic-themed online craft magazine, *The AntiCraft*. Stewart recounted how she learned to knit in 2002 by consulting a book rather than her grandmother.

Stewart regularly read the blog of a young woman who posted entries in both Spanish and English. When the bilingual blogger wrote about learning to knit, Stewart decided she wanted to learn, too.

"I thought, 'Wouldn't it be nice if my grandmother could teach me to knit?'" Stewart said. "She's Cuban. But she doesn't knit. But she gave me some money for my birthday, and I went out and got some hunter-orange yarn and a book."[8]

FROM THE CUTTING EDGE TO MIDDLE AMERICA

So far, our examination of the modern knitting revival's causes has focused on motivations of the knitting avant-garde. The DIY movement and third-wave feminism are driving the knitting craze, but a lot of re-liable, old-fashioned forces are at work, too. After all, one might legiti-mately ask why all these young, trendy folks chose knitting instead of another craft, like scrapbooking, sewing, or decoupage, as their leisure obsession. The answer lies in the nature of knitting, itself. We will look at knitting's special charms and how they appeal to modern lifestyles in Chapter 5.

5

A ROW OF ONE'S OWN: THE ENDURING CHARMS OF KNITTING

The knitting trend that emerged in the past decade is distinctive from other times when knitting returned to vogue. In the past, people knitted more when a need for garments or income arose, either because of war, sanctions on imports, or economic hardship. Today, knitting is popular with young women in spite of the expense it imposes. Knitting a sweater typically costs much more than buying one made with materials of comparable quality. Knitting is also a slow process. Making a sweater by hand requires many dozens of hours. And yet, in an era when spare time is rare and precious to most women, knitting is enjoying record-breaking popularity.

That's because knitting continues to fulfill needs that are rarely acknowledged or even named, though they are acute. Knitting satisfies needs for leisure, creativity, aesthetic and sensual stimulation, meditation, and contemplation. Knitting circles and online communities gratify the knitter with the pleasure of a community that appreciates one's talents and hard work. These needs had long been neglected by women in their twenties and thirties today, who focused most of their energy on trying to live the dream of their mothers and grandmothers: to be superwomen with great careers, happy and healthy families, beautiful bodies, and positive self-images. So many young women pursued all these noble goals, and then, like the housewives described in *The Feminine Mystique*, wondered what was missing from their lives.

Beyond third-wave feminism and the DIY movement, a common and perennial motivation for the urge to knit is the desire for personal gratification. Pleasure, happiness, playtime, and fun—these are some of the underappreciated but nonetheless essential elements of a full life that knitting provides. That's the dirty little secret that knitting has kept for its practitioners since it was invented. It is pleasure disguised as duty, play disguised as work.

The proof lies in the reasons that knitters give for their obsession with the craft. "It's a great way not to feel too guilty about watching TV," Joanne Muzzin of New Haven told me.[1]

Muzzin is a member of Stitch 'N Bitch New Haven, which includes several Yale students and graduates, as well as other college-educated professional women. Guilt over a lack of productivity was a theme among these knitters.

Another member of the circle, Jessica Lang, confessed guilt over idle hours spent commuting to her job in New York City, about two and a half hours away. Knitting on the train assuages that guilt, she said.[2]

Lauren Lax, a student at Yale School of Management, claimed that productivity was the main drive behind her compulsive knitting.[3] She minimizes costs by getting free yarn from manufacturers in exchange for designing or test-knitting patterns that companies sell. Lax has designed patterns for Lion Brand, a huge yarn company whose product is available at large craft stores. She has also invented styles for Alchemy Yarns of Transformation, a smaller maker of luxury yarns. Lax cannot keep items she makes with the free yarn. She sends them back to the yarn companies. The arrangement is fine with her, though. She is a process knitter. The product is less important to her than the knitting itself.

Other knitters cite a need to quell anxiety. In Philadelphia, Pennsylvania, the Knitters for Choice circle attracts many women in their twenties who are pursuing graduate degrees. The group raises money for women's health groups and clinics through the sale of hand knits. Elinore Kaufman, a postdoctoral premedical student at the University of Pennsylvania, hosts meetings at her apartment. She knits rapidly, rarely looking down at her work. Kaufman says she is fidgety and always needs to do something with her hands. She keeps herself busy. When not studying medicine, painting, or knitting, she volunteers at a needle-exchange program for heroin addicts.[4]

Knitting to ease tension or to occupy spare moments is nothing new. Women have enjoyed these benefits of the craft for centuries. Looking back one generation, I received a vivid description of knitting's more ambiguous and spiritual attributes from a fantastic knitter, weaver, and feminist of the second wave, Selma Miriam. In Bridgeport, Connecticut, Miriam hosts a multigenerational knitting circle each Wednesday at Bloodroot, the feminist vegetarian restaurant she has co-owned since the seventies.

"I'm a very impatient person," Miriam said. "I hear people say I don't have the patience to knit. I don't have the patience *not to knit* [italics added] because there's so many places where there's nothing to do."[5]

Knitting has kept her sane, she said. Once while in Brooklyn, New York, shopping for restaurant supplies, Miriam returned to her parking space to find her car missing. After some frantic phone calls, she learned the car had been towed to the Brooklyn Navy Yard. Getting it back would require figuring out the yard's location, getting herself there, and paying a hefty fine. When she finally found her vehicle, she had to wait with other unfortunates who had parked illegally.

"I sat down on the floor and took out my knitting," she said. "It's the only way I deal with stress. It's the only way to cope. It just makes everything possible. The purpose is not to have a sweater or a scarf. The purpose is to continue your life and not feel like life is horrific."

Knitting, like other creative arts, Miriam claims, involves transformation akin to magic. She believes the notion of transformation is particularly appealing to women. Miriam mentioned Native American author Paula Gunn Allen's description of magic as the art of transformation.

"'Ma,' mother, and 'gi,' Earth—magic is what the earth gives you," Miriam said. "When you take an egg and make an omelet, that's magic. When you take a piece of string and turn it into a sweater, that's magic."

"It's all about transformation. This is the kind of thing that women really get off on doing," Miriam said. "These kinds of things, the so-called domestic arts, that's why I think it's coming back, because people are hungry for it."

The theme of transformation came up again when, months later, I interviewed Stephanie Pearl-McPhee, writer of several humor titles and the popular knitting blog, Yarn Harlot. Pearl-McPhee also said she gets excited over the wonder of making beautiful, useful things out of sticks and string.

"I find the transformative aspect of it really compelling," Pearl-McPhee said. "I find the idea of turning one thing into another thing really compelling. I've often said that knitting is a modern magic trick."[6]

Pearl-McPhee is also a doula, guiding women through the physical and emotional aspects of childbirth. Maternity, the power of the female body to introduce a new life into the world, is also linked to women's interest in transformation, she said.

"I have a private list I keep of the names of people I've touched first," Pearl-McPhee said. "It's a profound and sacred thing. I try to live really well, in case I'm putting a mojo on them."

Transformation is a process essential to womanhood. "It's a biological imperative," Pearl-McPhee quipped, attributing her knitting and spinning obsession to the fact that she has enough children. "When one has had three kids, I think it's time you find another way of making things," she said. "Now I turn sheep into sweaters."

Some knitters claim that they concentrate better when they are knitting. They may take up their needles during classes, at church, while chatting with nonknitting friends, or even in board meetings.

Maria Alvarez, another member of Knitters for Choice in Philadelphia, says knitting helps her focus her thoughts. Alvarez is an art student and Starbuck's barista in her twenties who graduated from Swarthmore College with a science degree. She is fastidious about keeping her stitches nearly perfectly even. Alvarez would often knit during large, survey courses in college, holding her pen between her last two fingers and taking notes without ever dropping her needles.[7]

A surprising number of young women attested to knitting in college classes, including Suyen Lyn, a mother of two boys in New Rochelle, New York. Lyn took up knitting at Smith College in Northampton, Massachusetts, where, she said, knitting in class was commonplace.[8]

Not every professor appreciates students knitting during class, of course, and some forbid it. People who don't knit sometimes find the activity distracting and even impolite or offensive when it is done during other activities.

For instance, knitting during religious services can raise eyebrows. The female pastor of a rather liberal Lutheran church in Philadelphia asked if I noticed how some of her parishioners were knitting in the pews. She was loath to ask them to stop, but confided, "I sometimes wonder if I'm not interesting enough for them."

One knitting parishioner later said she thinks the pastor is coming to understand that many of them pay better attention when their hands are busy. In business or political settings, knitting can be interpreted as passive-aggressive or defiant.

Professional women may catch flak for knitting in nontraditional locales, like workplace cafeterias and board meetings. I can attest to several instances where people around a knitter voiced resentment of the knitter, specifically because of the knitting. Names are omitted to protect the knitters. I know of these situations either from my firsthand experience or because the knitters shared these stories with me.

A management consulting company was volunteering its services to an ad hoc committee of executives for two nonprofit organizations that were confidentially considering a merger. The consultants invited the committee to attend a two-hour meeting to review and discuss recommendations. One of the invited executives whipped out her knitting needles during the consultants' lengthy PowerPoint presentation. The consultants later expressed surprise and irritation that this female executive voiced so much criticism of their recommendations—which were given pro bono, they noted—when she couldn't be bothered to put down her needlework.

A panel of scientists was organized by the National Aeronautics and Space Administration (NASA) to review applications for grants. Among the panelists was a female astrophysicist, the recipient of NASA grants herself. She brought her knitting to these grant reviews. She participated in heated debates over the merits and flaws of various candidates' work, no doubt expressing her opinion forcefully, as she usually does. Colleagues at the table snickered and took to calling her Madame Defarge, after Charles Dickens' heartless character in *A Tale of Two Cities*, who vengefully works the names of her enemies, who will be executed during the French Revolution, into her knitting.

At a community hospital, a group of chaplains is discussing their day's rounds to patients wanting pastoral counseling. A female supervisor is reviewing how the chaplains' leader is facilitating the meeting, and she knits while she watches. The man under review is a Buddhist monk, and the local press has been critical of the hospital's choice of him, rather than, say, a Christian or Jewish cleric, to lead the team of chaplains. He is feeling the full weight of public scrutiny. After the meeting, and once the supervisor has departed, the monk concedes he felt distracted by and resentful of the incessant click, click, click of the supervisor's knitting needles. The team commiserates with their leader and shares their concern that the supervisor was not giving her full attention to their discussion.

Instances like these inspire artists like Freddie Robins, whose work will be discussed at greater length later in this chapter. Her work, *Craft Kills*, depicts the artist as Saint Sebastian, though knitting needles rather than arrows pierce her body.

Robins said she was inspired by how craft is seen as a benign, passive activity. She asked herself, "How would it be if it were actually a dangerous activity, if it was something we actually weren't allowed to do, if it was banned?"

"And then knitting was banned (after the terrorist attacks of September 11, 2001) from when you were flying," Robins said. "You couldn't fly and knit. And so knitting is seen as a dangerous activity when you're doing something else. That's what that piece is all about."[9]

KNITTING AS A SUBVERSIVE ACT

Some argue that public knitters are engaging in subversion. "I think you could say that knitting is a radical practice in a culture that is so compulsive about buying things," Cat Mazza, creator of microRevolt, in an interview with reporter Beth Rosenberg.[10]

Mazza considered gender issues when, in creating microRevolt, she deliberately used a male-dominated medium, computers, to mobilize knitters, traditionally a female group, against sweatshop labor. Female textile workers in the Northeast were among the first people to revolt against unfair labor practices and pay. She argues that knitters are naturally sympathetic to the cause of sweatshop labor because they understand the work that goes into making a garment.

In San Francisco, male knitter Jesse Loesberg, also known on his knitting Web site as Yarn Boy, has written about how men commit a subversive act by knitting in public. He broadcasted his views on radio station KQED-FM,[11] and he spoke more on the subject in an interview with me.

"I like that there's something about knitting that diffuses the natural tension among strangers," he said. "In this culture, we don't make a lot of eye contact with people we don't know. It's unusual to strike arbitrary conversations, and if a strange person does, that's usually greeted with a certain amount of suspicion. There's something about knitting that undercuts that, especially if you're a male knitter. People assume that you must be a really nice guy, which is in some instances true, I guess."[12]

Since the radio broadcast, Loesberg said he has become less happy about the attention that his public knitting draws. "The flip side is that people speak to me when I don't want to be spoken to," he said. "After a long day at work, I really like to knit on the long train ride home, and I really don't want to talk to anyone." (Loesberg stutters, so speaking is often stressful for him, he said.)

Loesberg's wife knits, too, and they often compare people's reactions to their knitting. "People will sometimes speak to her on the train, but only if she's knitting something fascinating, while I'm a fair target," he said. "Wearing headphones helps." Knitting leads some people to make other assumptions about Loesberg, he said.

"Once I was sitting in a café with a friend, who's a guy, and I was showing him how to knit," he said. "This woman came up to us and said, 'Oh! You guys are gay!' There was something off with her, but I know people are surprised that (1) I'm straight and (2) I'm married. That's happened for me for most of my adult life, aside from the knitting. I seem to have a lot of the social signs and signifiers that say, 'gay.' If you are a reasonably attractive guy already, there's going to be a lot of eye contact with other men, and knitting opens the door for that."

Mazza views knitting as subversive because it defies the common values of our age—speed, consumption, and convenience. Loesberg calls male knitting subversive because it rejects gender stereotypes and, thus, invites others to set aside social rules against interacting with strangers in public places. Some other knitters are subversive for what they do with their knitting and how that knitting challenges the assumptions of the people who view it.

In Montrose, Texas, a trendy section of Houston, a gang of young mothers subverts two genres, knitting and graffiti, by "tagging" lamp posts, car antennae, door handles, and trees with their colorful bits of hand-knit fabric.[13] In the world of graffiti artists, a tag is a graffiti logo or signature that the vandal typically spray paints someplace in public view. These knitting graffiti artists call their posse "Knitta, Please!"—the name is a play on an Ol' Dirty Bastard song that uses a pejorative term against black people—and each member adopts a moniker such as AKrylik, PolyCotN, P-Knitty, LoopDog, or WoolFool. Unlike spray paint, their knitted graffiti is easy to remove. Knitta gang members affix their tags with buttons.

The group has taken their fluffy vandalism on the road, and they have also inspired the spread of knitted graffiti in other cities. Their Web site, www.myspace.com/knittaplease includes a collage of knitted graffiti sightings that have hailed from as far away from Texas as the Great Wall of China.

Sabrina Gschwandtner, a fiber artist, curator of knitting and crochet exhibitions, and founder of the fiber arts magazine *KnitKnit*, described how Knitta's tags function as art, because they subvert common notions about knitting and graffiti.[14]

Gschwandtner photographed Knitta's graffiti on the Williamsburg Bridge in lower Manhattan, where security is tight following the terrorist attacks of September 11, 2001.

"Lower Manhattan is a completely surveyed site right now," Gschwandtner said. "Cops are everywhere. We were there at 5 P.M. on the Manhattan side of the Williamsburg Bridge. There were several cops standing nearby directing traffic. In New York City you have to have a permit to publicly photograph anything if you're obviously not a tourist. They're very tough about it. We hadn't gotten a permit. Also, if you photograph the bridge it can raise suspicion."

A cop approached the photographer and the knitted graffiti and asked, "What is this?" Gschwandtner, interested in what the officer's response to the graffiti would be, pretended to be clueless.

"The cop started musing on the knitted graffiti," Gschwandtner recalled. He said it was interesting. He pondered how it got there, why it was there, and whether it would stay there or get removed.

"I'd be really interested to see what happens," the officer told Gschwandtner. Had the graffiti been spray painted, the artist speculated, it would have been removed immediately.

THE EFFECTS OF SEPTEMBER 11, 2001

Anyone can see that the terrorist attacks on the World Trade Center and the Pentagon on September 11, 2001 had shattering effects on

Americans and people around the world, particularly the people of Afghanistan and Iraq. More than 3,000 people died in New York City on that day, and thousands more are dying in related warfare. Those Americans who are not in the military have seen their lives changed. We are more fearful. We are watching our civil rights shrink while the rights of visitors to our country dissolve even faster.

Some people have asked if knitting is popular because of the events of September 11, 2001. Sadly, I think it more likely that bigotry is gaining popularity in America because of the evil, devastating acts of a few fanatics on that day.

Certainly, some knitters comforted themselves with their hobby following the attacks. Lucia Herndon, who was a columnist for *The Philadelphia Inquirer* at the time, wrote about her surge in knitting then. She also got letters from readers who said they, too, became attached to the craft after September 11.

"Several readers have contacted me relating tales of knitting far into the night, of nonstop knitting, knitting to calm their tattered nerves. One self-described habitual knitter 'has become an obsessive knitter' since that horrible day."

Herndon wrote about a woman who set aside knitting for twenty years but, after September 11, felt "compelled" to knit a scarf for her daughter in red, white, and blue. The woman told Herndon that she was surprised at the ferocity with which she knit, staying up late into the night. "There was something very comforting about the sound of the needles." Herndon quoted the woman as saying.[15] Suss Cousins, a knitter for Hollywood films and knitting teacher to celebrities, says in her book *Hollywood Knits Style* that after the attacks she saw demand for her knitting classes triple.

"These days people definitely feel the need to be together and to do something special for family and friends, both near and faraway," Cousins wrote.[16]

Without a doubt, knitters could have found some solace in the meditative quality of knitting, and some people who longed to relax or console themselves picked up their knitting needles. People probably leaned on their other comforts more than usual as well. They may have overeaten or gotten drunk more often. They may have done more yoga or taken more baths. They no doubt hugged their kids more often for a while.

And yet, if all people sought from knitting were relief from pain and fear, they would have stopped knitting by now. Knitting, just like other addictive behaviors, would prove a woefully inadequate salve. It happens, too, that the knitting revival was burgeoning before September 11, 2001. No knitter I have interviewed attributed the knitting trend to that infamous day, and a few have brought up that theory only to refute it. Loesberg discredits the idea.

"I've heard some people say it's because of September 11," Loesberg said. "I don't believe that. September 11 changed a lot of things, but it didn't change everything. I don't think that every significant trend now goes back to that."[17] Stephanie Pearl-McPhee of Yarn Harlot fame rejected all theories that forces beyond the joy of knitting itself had encouraged the knitting trend.

"People ask me all the time why knitting is so popular," Pearl-McPhee said. "I say, 'Really, because it's fun and it's interesting.' Then they say, 'No, really. Is it feminism?' I say, 'No, I don't think it's feminism.' They say, 'Is it because people are searching for something real in a fast-moving world? Is it a reaction to the events of 9/11 and a need for security?'"

Pearl-McPhee asserts that people knit for more basic reasons. "It comes down to, 'It's really fun, and it's really interesting,'" she said.[18] "Think about it," she said. "When you show someone your knitting, do they say, 'Oh, my God, this is meeting so many of my feminist needs!' or do they say, 'Wow. That's really cool.'?"

Pearl-McPhee also said she's not convinced that knitting's popularity has really surged all that much. She believes instead that knitting is getting more media attention as people knit more often in public and write about knitting on blogs. The media and word-of-mouth publicity are, in turn, piquing the curiosity of some new knitters, she contends.

"A lot of what's happening is that knitters are coming out of the closet," Pearl-McPhee said. "Knitters are hooking up. They're getting together in public, because it's a more social thing, something you don't do by yourself. And the rest of them are seeing how much fun we're having."

"I also think it makes people feel smart," Pearl-McPhee added. "Have you ever knit a sock?" When I answered that, in fact, no, I had never knitted a sock—I was afraid of the challenge the heel presents—she scoffed (and contradicted herself slightly), insisting that I could do it. I could knit a sock. One-on-one, Pearl-McPhee is even funnier than her blog and books indicate. "Afraid of a sock?" she asked incredulously. "Be afraid of al Qaeda. Be afraid of global warming." She listed several other items worthy of my fear, including things like pandemics and sociopathic world leaders who wage unnecessary wars. "Don't be afraid of a sock!" she said.

Despite the fuzzy and non-threatening nature of her chosen hobby, Pearl-McPhee insisted that September 11, 2001 did not spur the knitting trend. In any case, the reader of these pages is encouraged to decide for herself what is motivating modern knitters.

CELEBRITY KNITTERS

Knitting's current popularity coincides with many media sightings of celebrities knitting. Those said to knit include Madonna, Sandra

Bullock, Cameron Diaz, Kate Moss, Hilary Swank, Brooke Shields, Daryl Hannah, Julia Roberts, Goldie Hawn, Uma Thurman, and Mary-Louise Parker. Movie stars are not the only famous folk knitting in public, either. Former U.S. Secretary of State Madeleine Albright is also a knitter.

Some trickster even mocked up a picture of Russell Crowe fumbling with knitting needles, and the image was circulated on the Internet. No proof was offered that the Hollywood bad boy actually knits.

Hollywood filmmakers in recent years have commissioned hand-knit items to be worn on screen by their leading actors in films such as *Chicken Run*, *Harry Potter and the Philosopher's Stone*, and *Cider House Rules*.[19]

Edith Eig, owner of La Knitterie Parisienne yarn shop in Studio City, California, has made a name for herself as a knit designer for films and knitting teacher to the stars. In response to the terrorist attacks of September 11, 2001, Eig organized famous actors to knit blankets that were auctioned to benefit the New York Police and Fire Widows' and Children's Fund.[20] Eig even hosted the television program, *Knit One, Purl Two*, on the DIY Network. The success of that show was so great that the channel established a regular program on knitting, *Knitty Gritty*, hosted by Vicki Howell. In 2005, BBC News even attributed a boom in yarn sales in the United Kingdom to the apparent surge in Hollywood knitters.[21]

Left: Cat Mazza with stitched knitPro sign, 2005. Courtesy of Cat Mazza.

Right: Maria Alvarez of Philadelphia's Knitters for Choice knits a dog sweater. Photo by author.

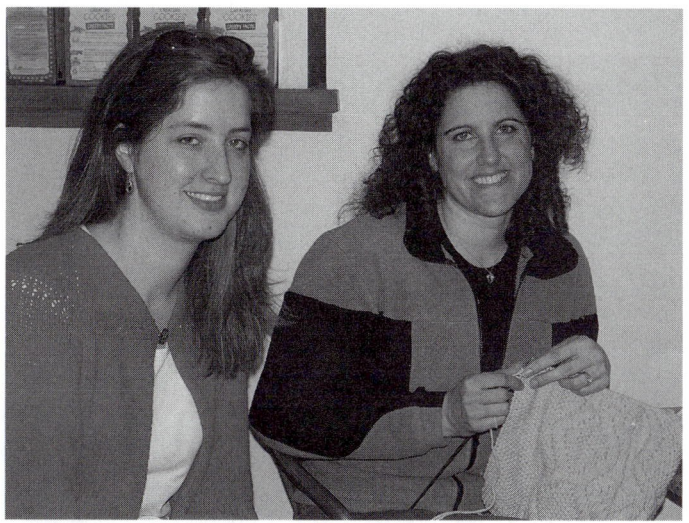

Members of Stitch 'N Bitch New Haven meet at a local restaurant. Photo by author.

Top: Jesse Loesberg, creator of the Web site, Yarn Boy, knits with his wife Zoë Gladstone in their San Francisco home. Reprinted with permission from Loesberg's Web site, Yarn Boy.

Bottom Left: Artist Sabrina Gschwandtner is helping to change the image of knitted art. Photo by Chris Habib. Courtesy of Sabrina Gschwandtner.

Bottom Right: Freddie Robins with a tea cozy from her work, "Knitted Homes of Crime." The collection features the houses of women who kill, or the houses in which those women committed murder. Photo by Peter Sharpe.

Knitters from all walks of life gather at The Tangled Web, a yarn store in Philadelphia's Mount Airy neighborhood. Photo by author.

A knitter celebrates completion of a challah bread cover, with the bread blessing knitted in Hebrew onto it, by sharing a loaf with friends at The Tangled Web. Photo by author.

Lauren Lax and Jennifer Wang at a New Haven Stitch 'N Bitch meeting. Lax is trying on a sweater she has almost finished knitting without a pattern. Photo by author.

Members of Knitters for Choice gather for a tea party in a member's home. Photo by author.

Left: An American in Paris: Kate Gilbert sits at a Paris café wearing Clapotis, the scarf she designed for the online magazine, *Knitty*. Clapotis is probably the most famous free knitting pattern in the world today. Photo by Fred Gilbert. Courtesy of Kate Gilbert.

Right: Renée Rigdon (left) and Zabet Stewart (right) fear the camera. Here is a caricature of the pair, drawn by Rigdon's husband, Matt Rigdon. Courtesy Stewart and Rigdon.

Rachael Herron, writer of the blog, Yarn-A-Go-Go, and Lala Hulse on their honeymoon. They met on the Internet. Photographer unknown. Courtesy Rachael Herron.

A woman spins angora fur into yarn directly off the bunny at the Maryland Sheep and Wool Festival, a kind of Mecca for diehard knitters and spinners. Photo by author.

6

ART IN THE CRAFT: HOW FINE FIBER ARTISTS EXPLOIT THE MEDIUM

On the far end of subversive knitting are several innovative fiber artists. Sabrina Gschwandtner, a New York City artist, curator, and founder of the fiber arts magazine *KnitKnit* said knitting becomes art, "when it takes some kind of risk, when it questions its function, when it pushes the form to an extreme and causes you to think conceptually, to push your thinking."[1] "Craft is typically defined as being explicitly made to function," Gschwandtner said. "Art is something that questions function or has made you question something."

The line between art and craft can get pretty fuzzy when one chooses to work with yarn as a medium or knitting or crocheting as a genre. Furthermore, art tends to get more respect than craft does. Gschwandtner explained why some fine artists today consider working with fiber as a medium worth the risk to their reputations.

"Personally, I just was really excited about the texture, the color, all the same reasons any artist chooses the materials they work with," Gschwandtner said. "Part of the act of making art, the reason you commit yourself to doing it forever, is that you're drawn to material and seeing what you can do with it."

Gschwandtner was a designer of knitted and crocheted fashion for Henri Bendel before she decided to pursue a career in fine art. At Brown University, she had studied film and video and semiotics, and these subjects, combined with her interest in knitting and crochet, inform her artwork. Her art includes installations that incorporate film, video, crochet, and sewing. She also creates single channel works, which are shown during screenings and festivals, where the viewer must watch the work from beginning to end.

In 2002, Gschwandtner founded *KnitKnit*, a biannual publication that features articles, interviews, profiles, illustrations, and reviews. "*KnitKnit* was about getting together people who come from an art background like me who were into knitting and crocheting," Gschwandtner said.

Limited edition copies of each issue have handmade covers created by a fine artist. In a sense, these copies of the magazine are works of art in themselves. They have been exhibited at museums and galleries, including the Baltimore Museum of Art and the Center for Contemporary Art in Rotterdam. *KnitKnit* can also be purchased in select bookstores and yarn shops.

Many other artists are also exploring the intersection of art and craft through knitting. Jamie Petersen, a San Francisco knitter, contemplated the usefulness of knitting when she began cutting plastic grocery bags into spirals of ribbon, then tied them together to knit bags out of them.[2] Her project, Bags from Bags, caught the attention of artists and knitters when excerpts of a conversation with her were published in *KnitKnit*. Petersen said she got the idea to make bags from bags when she was fiddling with a piece of cellophane wrap that packaged a sandwich she ate. She crocheted a bracelet out of the plastic, and then she mused on what other projects she could invent to make use of waste.

"The idea with the bags is to just get them out there, so people can use them and be inspired to make their own or think about the material in a new way—as useful and not wasteful," Petersen told *KnitKnit*. "I sometimes fantasize about producing a grocery bag machine that would automatically cut the bags and then knit them, but I think that if the handbags were mass-produced, they would make more plastic bags just to make the handbags. The machine would defeat its own purpose."

The primary purpose of Petersen's project is to make people think. Is her knitting art rather than craft? In *KnitKnit*, Petersen considers the question. She cites an interview that PBS journalist Charlie Rose conducted with the controversial artist Richard Serra, whose most famous work, *Piss Christ*, is a figure of Jesus in a bottle filled with yellow liquid.

In the Rose interview, Serra argued that objects with a function could not be art. Petersen said the comment distressed her, coming from an artist as innovative as Serra. Petersen saw a flaw in his logic.

"After thinking about it I decided that art has a function, too," Petersen said. "If its purpose is to be useless, then it still has a purpose, meaning it still functions in some way if a person is experiencing its uselessness. So I guess Serra's categories don't make sense to me, and ultimately I disagree with his idea."

Others believe that knitting can be art, but only if it functions purely as art—not also as a useful object. In the United Kingdom, the Crafts Council of London capitalized on the knitting craze to mount an exhibit of knitted objects in February and May of 2005. The co-curator for the show, Knit 2 Together: Concepts in Knitting, was Freddie Robins, a fiber artist educated at the Royal College of Art. (Katie Bevins also co-curated.) Robins' work is widely viewed as subversive. She chose to include in the show only knitting without practical functions.

Among these works was Marie Rose Lortet's *Veste Pour Oiseaux Migratures (Jacket for a Migrating Bird)*. Though the work is a jacket, an item that normally serves a function, it is too tiny to be worn. Lortet knitted it on miniscule needles, making up the pattern as she went along, using patchwork and wild colors.

San Franciscan fine artist Andy Diaz Hope, who sometimes works in knitting, included a piece in the show, a city suit with knitted accessories like ski masks and epaulets that is part of his series, *Everybody is Somebody's Terrorist*. Other pieces in the series depict religious people and men outfitted in standard terrorist garb. Robins said Diaz Hope's work was the most overtly political in the show.

Janet Morton, a Canadian artist, covered all the items in a living room in Aran knitted fabric, including a fan, phone, and vacuum. "This talks about the obsessive nature of knitting and the coziness of knitting," Robins said on Marie Irshad's knitting podcast, KnitCast. "It takes that to a real extreme."[3]

Welsh artist Kelly Jenkins used an industrial machine designed to knit fine t-shirt fabric to make the kind of sex advertisements that are often seen inside telephone booths in the United Kingdom. Robins said the work juxtaposes the benign image of knitting against the seediness of the sex industry.

Robins' own creations are clever examples of how knitting can be used to make people think. Her works are particularly successful in exploring ideas about gender, the body, and domesticity.

"Lots of things I like to talk about in my work are issues of abnormality and conformity," Robins said in an interview with this author.[4] "Knitting is such a friendly medium that I can talk about sort of difficult things with it. I suppose that's what I mean when I describe it as subversive. It's like tricking people into things. You can really talk about anything."

Knitted Homes of Crime, is a prime example of how Robins can exploit her medium to provoke examination of human prejudices. The 2002 installation featured machine-knitted and embroidered tea cozies, which, in typical Victorian fashion, were designed to look like houses. But these cozies were carefully modeled after the homes of real women who committed murders or the places where they killed.

The artist collapses several symbols of femininity: knitting, the home, and tea—in a cozy, no less—to depict places where the utmost evil occurred. It's art, and it's also very crafty.

In the December 2005 interview with Marie Irshad on KnitCast, Robins described her intentions further. "Women (killers) are always seen as doubly deviant because they've committed a crime and they've gone against their nature," Robins said. "To society it seems much worse than a man committing a crime. And I used playing that off against knitting and what knitting is usually used for: it's used to make something comforting and cozy, nurturing."

Robins researched the murders on which she based her art and found that many of the women used poison to kill. Robins saw this as an interesting twist: by providing a drink—perhaps tea—or food to their victims, they disguised their crime within the performance of a conventionally female duty. "Again, they're using their nurturing, but to evil ends," Robins said.

"I find knitting to be a powerful medium for self-expression because of the cultural preconceptions surrounding it," Robins states on her Web site. "My work subverts these preconceptions and disrupts the notion of the medium being passive and benign."

Other of Robins' works grapple with ideas about physical normality. She designs garments with distorted elements, like sweaters with extra-long arms or no holes for hands to peek through, arm sleeves where necks should be, or socks at the ends of sleeves.

"They talk about the supposedly normal body," Robins told Irshad. "I'm exploring issues of what that might be, why we're meant to look a certain way, what is it with trying to make people perfect, and standardization. I even had one comment from someone saying, it's such a shame no one can wear them. And I was saying, 'Yeah, that's the point!'"

On the Web site for London's Victoria and Albert Museum, where some of the oldest-known pieces of knitted fabric are displayed, a pattern designed by Robins is available for download. It is for a pair of gray gloves, the left hand of which is mutilated. The thumb extends only to the knuckle. Red sprays of yarn imitate blood, for a horrific effect.[5]

The introduction to the pattern explains the inspiration for this artwork, designed by Robins and hand knitted by Jean Arkell, which is part of the museum's collections.

> Freddie Robins' subversive knitting includes a series of gloves where pairs join, single gloves have ten fingers or each finger sprouts a new glove. "Conrad" is a character from the nineteenth century book of cautionary tales, *Struwwelpeter*, by Dr. Heinrich Hoffmann. Conrad's mother

warns Conrad that if he continues to suck his thumbs the scissor-man will come and cut them off. He ignores her warnings and, "Snip! Snap! Snip!" he loses his thumbs.

One of Robins' exhibits featured a short-sleeved sweater she made for Mat Fraser, a man whose arms were deformed in a birth defect caused by the drug, thalidomide. The sweater's chest bears the words, "Short-armed and dangerous!"[6]

October 2005 marked the delightful convergence of high art and popular culture through the act of knitting. Robins called on a renegade London knitting club called Cast Off[7] to take up residence at London's Pump House Gallery during an exhibit called *Ceremony*, which considered rites of passage and what craft has to do with them. Robins doubled as curator and bride for the wedding. Everything— bridal gown, tea, sandwiches, flowers, confetti, cake, and even those doves that really ambitious couples like to release at their nuptials— was knitted. Cast Off chose the wedding as their theme because, though it isn't necessarily the most important rite of passage, it's the one on which most people spend the most time and money.

Cast Off posted a call for knitted wedding accoutrements on its Web site, urging contributors not to worry about the quality of their contributions. Cast Off provided patterns for several knitted wedding items, including candles, flowers, and canapés.

Robins said she has battled with the medium of knitting over the years. She learned the craft from her godmother, a strong female figure in her life. "I was trained in textile design early on, and I presumed I would work more as a designer," Robins said. She switched to fine art because she recognized that the meaning of the work was important to her, and she wanted to be more expressive.

"I've tried ditch it," Robins said of knitting. She detested the traditional associations people make with knitting and knitters. On the other hand, her love of the craft was too strong to resist. "I physically love it," she said. "I engage with it. I couldn't go against it so I decided I would work with it and everything it brought."

Robins' interest in challenging ideas about gender has become more acute since the birth of her daughter in 2004. "All the issues I thought had been dealt with . . . aren't," Robins said. "Having a two-year-old daughter really brought it home to me even more." Ideas about differences between the sexes and whether they are innate or taught, about what girls or boys are naturally good at, "have been thrown in my face," she said.

An American artist has also begun to explore gender through knitting with his knitted costumes for superheroes. Using himself as a mannequin, Arizona State University art professor Mark Newport spent about two months on each of his creations. *Super Heroic* at the Arizona State University Art Museum from June to September 2005 was Newport's largest exhibition of his artwork when it opened. Since then, his works have been exhibited at several other venues across the country.

"Turning the superhero inside out is a way for me to present an understanding of masculinity," Newport said. "Superheroes suggest strength, but knitting them or covering them with embroidery provides a softness that is contradictory to their image."[8]

Another American fine artist who uses knitting as a medium is Lisa Anne Auerbach of Los Angeles, California. Auerbach, who studied photography while earning an M.F.A. at Art Center College of Design in Pasadena, is best known for making forceful political statements on knitwear. "Freedom is Messy," reads the front of a red and white sash. The back says, "Shoot to Kill."[9]

Another sweater carries a joke on its front: "Did you hear what Bush said when asked about Roe vs. Wade?" A small, gray fetus in utero is also depicted. On the back of the garment is the punch line: "I don't care how they get out of New Orleans." Auerbach notes on her Web site, "Some jokes aren't funny."

She also discusses on the site how she adopted the notion of sweater as canvas. During the seventies' heyday of the pop rock band Cheap Trick, front man Rick Nielsen wore custom-made sweaters bearing quirky statements like, "Don't Steal My Girlfriend." Those sweaters fueled Auerbach's imagination. She was interested in "the friction between the permanence of the material and the liveliness of the language and content." A sweater might last generations, but the message on it could lose relevance on the day the garment was made, she noted.

Auerbach brilliantly exploited that contrast between the durable and the ephemeral in her *Body Count* mittens. Adapting a traditional Scandinavian design, Auerbach knitted the number of American soldiers killed in Iraq by March 23, 2005 into the first mitten: 1,524. A week later, on March 31, she completed the second mitten, and the number of slain soldiers had risen to 1,533. Auerbach documented that number in the second mitten.

On the Web site for her knitted art, Stealthissweater.com, Auerbach provides a free pattern for the mittens. "This makes an excellent project to knit in public," Auerbach notes on the pattern. "It's small and portable, and the intricate-looking mittens attract attention and encourage conversation both about the knitting and the occupation/war."

She also includes with the pattern sources for up-to-date estimates of the number of soldiers killed and wounded. In August 2005, Auerbach made a *Body Count* sweater, which documented the number of Iraqi civilians killed.

An exploration of knitting history showed us how women used knitting to participate in political and wartime discourses while remaining in the domestic realm. Today, Auerbach's knitting criticizes the war, Newport's superheroes challenge ideas about masculinity, and Robins' works deconstruct our assumptions about knitting, womanhood, domesticity, and the normal body.

These artists, just like their knitting predecessors, are exploiting a fundamental truth about knitting: it is stretchy. Knitting can accommodate all kinds of people and a breathtaking variety of agendas.

7

THE KNITTING CIRCLE: SOCIAL AND CHARITABLE ASPECTS OF THE CRAFT

In the last chapter, we saw how versatile knitting is, how it can be manipulated to serve so many purposes and allow for individual expression. Here, we will look at another essential trait of knitting: its binding power. Knitting brings people together, and not just the people you might think. A love of knitting is the foundation for millions of human relationships, including unlikely ones.

Consider, for instance, the knitting community surrounding Rachael Herron. She is a thirty-four-year-old emergency dispatcher in Oakland, California, with an M.F.A. in writing from Mills College. She is also a blogger, and through her blog, Yarn-A-Go-Go, she has made hundreds of friends across the country. Herron wrote on her blog about her courtship and marriage to another Oakland woman, Lala Hulse. Though she has 140,000 readers since starting her blog in 2001, Herron has not received one gay-bashing comment. She remarked on this, knowing that, "sometimes, for these Midwestern women who read my blog (they) don't know a lesbian, and they'll write notes."

Herron once received an e-mail from just such a reader. "She wanted to know how she should approach her daughter, who she thought was gay," Herron said. "That was a really important e-mail. I took a lot of time to write that e-mail. The knitting has made me a gay emissary among some bloggers."

This sort of bonding between people of different backgrounds is not unique to knitters who meet using the Internet. At a knit-in event at The Tangled Web, a Philadelphia yarn shop, I saw a delightful convergence of cultures take place. While the shop owner poured wine for knitters, one of them pulled out her show-and-tell item, a knitted bread cover that bore a Hebrew blessing knitted into it. To celebrate completion of the cover, she had tucked a loaf of warm challah beneath it for the knitters to share.

This gift invited a host of questions from fellow knitters, mostly about knitting. How long did the lace edging take? What yarn was used? How would she wash it? But other questions revolved around Judaism. Was the bread always covered? What did the Hebrew inscription mean in English? And, from a genuinely inquisitive African American woman in her seventies, what does "Oy, gevult" mean?

Knitting circles across America routinely bring together young and old people, gays and straights, blacks, whites, Asians and Hispanics, those who speak English and those who do not, conservatives and liberals, men and women, and all kinds of folks who, if it weren't for the knitting, might just assume to avoid each other. Because they know from the start that they share a consuming passion, they are often able to look beyond their differences and think about what else they might have in common.

As is the case with so many aspects of knitting, the binding power of modern knitting circles is not an innovation. Knitting has always invited people to sit still together for hours at a time and get to know each other.

The knitting circle has been around for centuries because knitting is such a handy diversion for busy people. Knitting is portable and can usually be easily set aside and resumed, so it lends itself well to social gatherings. Another reason so many knitters join circles is that they can learn new techniques from each other. Live demonstrations are often easier to understand and repeat than instructions in books.

The reasons women knit together have not changed much, but the nature of knitting circles has. Over the ages, knitting circles typically gathered at predictable and relatively isolated locales, such as private homes and church halls. Modern knitters are changing this. They may meet in bustling cafes and bars, in parks, yarn stores, libraries, bookshops, and restaurants. A knitting circle in the United Kingdom called Cast Off makes a point of knitting in public and sometimes raises the ire of onlookers and public officials. The club even got kicked out of The American Bar at The Savoy, a swanky London hotel.[1]

Cast Off leader Rachael Matthews told a reporter for *The Guardian* that she wants to reclaim knitting as a positive social force. Knitting circles have always been strongly linked to oral tradition, and Matthews told a London reporter she believes that's because, "When you are knitting, you are ready to listen."[2]

Public knitting also becomes social because it attracts attention. Bemused non-knitters steal glances or approach and ask questions when they see women whose hair is not yet grey wielding knitting needles.

Some young people look on in envy, coveting the fascinating skills, the sumptuous yarns, and the easy friendships that knitters can enjoy.

By knitting in public, the craft's latest recruits subvert stereotypes. Onlookers can see that men and women knit. Some knitters are young, and some are old. Some are trendy, while some appear more matronly or traditional. Some knit afghans and baby blankets. Others knit lingerie or bikinis. And if you eavesdrop on conversations within a knitting circle, you're bound to get an earful. Some of it will be foreign to the non-knitter—there's talk of increases and yarn overs, intarsia and entrelac, dps, and pssos. Other conversations—about politics, sex, movies, books, sports, or work hassles—might seem familiar. When the curious recognize themselves among the knitters, the knitting circle grows.

The notion of knitters as grandmotherly and traditional women originated when knitting was a necessity, required to save money on clothing and, sometimes, to satisfy wartime needs for soldiers' garments. Typically, women fulfilled the need for knit items, and older family members taught younger ones how to knit.

The memory of those times haunted women who, in the sixties and seventies, took on new roles within the family. Second-generation feminists documented the changing attitude toward domestic work. Wives and mothers with paying jobs had less time to spare than money, so they were more apt to buy a sweater than make one. They sometimes remembered the knitting of their mothers and grandmothers as drudgery, so they shunned it.

"My mother loved to sew, loved to knit. I just didn't want to do that," British podcaster Marie Irshad said in her KnitCast interview of knitting artist Freddie Robins.[3] "I rebelled, saw it as being something domestic, which is such a shame looking back now, but there was that attitude about."

"Definitely," Robins responded. "My mother grew up in the war, so the last thing she wanted to do was knit and sew because she was forced to do that during the war. So when the war was over, she wanted to be a modern woman and go out and buy clothes."

Knitters under the age of forty are no less eager to be modern and free. The very fact that knitting is unnecessary and even indulgent enhances its allure. In an interview with this author, knitting podcaster Brenda Dayne of Cast On identified the latest wave of knitters as "solidly middle class . . . maybe even upper middle class." The abundance of novelty and luxury yarns, which typically cost more than basic acrylics, is fueling the movement. Knitting is a luxury hobby—one that requires a little extra money and time. And that's why women are enjoying it, suggests Dayne. "If it were still necessary, then there wouldn't be the sort of glamour around it," Dayne said. "Because we don't need to do it, we choose to do it."

Fiber artist Sabrina Gschwandtner sees the phenomenon similarly. "Thirty or forty years ago (knitting's) function was to provide garments," Gschwandtner said. "It doesn't have that function anymore. It can be to get together with friends, or to do it while you're waiting to download something from your computer, or while you wait for the subway, or it can be because you want to make your own clothes."[4]

Just as knitters knit for different reasons, they also gather into circles to support a variety of needs. Many newer knitters identify with Debbie Stoller's ideas and align with her under the Stitch 'N Bitch moniker. Still more go by other names or no name at all. Some may choose to knit for a cause. Other knitters look for circles whose members share a common interest besides knitting.

"I NEEDED FRIENDS"

Jennifer Wang is a twenty-six-year-old quality engineer for Schick, the razor company. She was born in Taiwan, and then lived in California for a decade before going to college in upstate New York.[5] When she moved to New Haven, Connecticut for a job, she went online to look for friends with similar interests. That's where she found out about New Haven Stitch 'N Bitch, a group of young knitters who meet twice a week in local eateries. "I found it because I needed friends," Wang said.

THERE'S ALWAYS GOING TO BE A BETTER KNITTER

"The best thing about a knitting group is getting ideas," said Bryna Subherwal,[6] a twenty-nine-year-old member of Stitch 'N Bitch New Haven. "If you're stuck, there's always going to be someone who's a better knitter."

Subherwal said their club's super knitter is Lauren Lax,[7] a business student at Yale who finagles much of her yarn for free by designing and test-knitting patterns for yarn companies. Lax persuaded many women in her knitting circle to start their own blogs. When I visited the circle, Lax and Wang were trying out the same patternless technique for knitting a sweater in the round, in the way that knitting legend Elizabeth Zimmermann would have had them do it.

"A HIDDEN PLACE"

A knitting circle meets weekly at Bloodroot, a feminist vegetarian restaurant in Bridgeport, Connecticut's eclectic Black Rock neighborhood. Bloodroot began hosting women knitters long before the current knitting craze. Co-owner Selma Miriam is an expert knitter and weaver. Woven tapestries hang from the rafters over the dining room. In a rear corner, a bookshop is filled with not only feminist and gay and lesbian literature but with many books on needlecrafts, as well as handspun yarns and other knitting and spinning notions. A slate patio outside is home to cats and an herb garden. The place takes visitors back to the heyday of second-wave feminism when Bloodroot opened its doors in 1975.

Thirty-year-old Jennifer Koenig wasn't even born then. Even so, she is a regular at the Wednesday night knitting circle. Recently married and just starting up her own daycare business, Koenig says coming to Bloodroot for a meatless meal and camaraderie is nearly essential for her.

"I feel comfortable here," Koenig said. "I feel instantly comfortable and warm—no stress, no pressure, no expectations. I get to meet new people. It's almost like a retreat from the real world, almost like I'm in a hidden place."[8]

CONNECTING WITH OLDER KNITTERS

Unlike many Stitch 'N Bitch gatherings, which tend to attract mostly younger knitters, Bloodroot's knitting circle attracts members of many ages. It also includes a few men. The broad age range is viewed as an asset among members.

Koenig clearly adores Miriam. The younger woman said she imagines that her own grandmother was a lot like Miriam. Koenig never got to know her grandmother, who died of a neurological illness when Koenig was seventeen. And yet, Koenig's mother described to her a vigorous, political, and opinionated woman—the kind of woman Miriam is and Koenig would like to be.

Koenig explained how she came to Bloodroot and to knitting as part of a path toward greater authenticity in her life. The young woman was working, unhappily, for a local pharmaceutical company and then, as a meeting planner. When those jobs proved unfulfilling, Koenig began to study experiential health and healing. Her coursework required her to find two mentors, and she chose Miriam as one of them. Not only did Koenig come regularly to knitting sessions, but she also visited Miriam's home and worked in her garden.

Koenig inherited her grandmother's knitting needles, but she only started using them when she met Miriam. Though she had been knitting for months, Koenig was still working on her first project when I met her: a long, red scarf in a small gauge, on which she had meticulously attempted dozens of complex stitch patterns. She tossed the scrolled scarf open across one of Bloodroot's long, planked tables. It unfurled like a narrow red carpet, welcoming her grandmother into her life. "I really wanted to knit because it would make me feel close to her," Koenig said. "When I hold the needles, I remember she held them."

I was surprised by how many young knitters I encountered who described a similar sense of connection to older knitters through the inheritance of knitting needles. Jesse Loesberg, a San Francisco knitter and writer who publishes the Web site Yarn Boy, described how he inherited a set of needles from his grandmother.[9]

"My grandmother knit. She died in January 2002. I learned in 2000, so I was only knitting during the last few years of her life. She was really thrilled I had learned to knit, but she was not the one who taught me," Loesberg said. "One thing is that her collection of needles and notions was vast, and it's mine. It's really special. I try to knit on her needles (exclusively). I like the metal, the way the yarn slides on it. What's really special is that my grandmother's hands were on these needles."

Lax, of New Haven Stitch 'N Bitch, also treasures a full set of needles given to her by an ex-boyfriend's grandmother—the woman who taught her to knit. "I miss her," Lax said as she showed me the set, kept in a calico needle case hand-sewn by the elder woman.

A white pitcher full of colorful metal needles graces the masthead of the popular online knitting magazine, *Knitty*. Those are editor Amy Singer's inheritance from her own grandmother, Lillian Balaban Goldstein Bernstein. Singer opens up about her grandmother in the maiden issue of *Knitty*. When her grandmother died, Singer took home her needles and, a year later, she discovered that knitting with them made her feel better. Until using those needles, quilting was Singer's main craft. "I hadn't realized the comfort and solace knitting provided me," Singer wrote. "I realize it now. Quilting feels like work but knitting is like breathing."[10]

KNIT YOUR BIT

Knitting may not be necessary, but lots of people who knit use the craft as a way to fulfill the needs of others. Circles spring up around myriad causes.

Knitters for Choice is a circle that meets monthly in members' homes around Philadelphia. They knit items that they sell to raise money for women's health organizations. NARAL and the Women's Medical Fund of Philadelphia have both received donations from the club. The group was founded by Farrah Parkes, a former Philly resident who lives in Princeton, New Jersey. Today Elinore Kaufman leads Knitters for Choice. Kaufman is a post-doctoral pre-medical student at the University of Pennsylvania.

Like Bloodroot's knitting circle, Knitters for Choice includes women from a wide array of disciplines, but most are young. Many are in their twenties, newly graduated from college and in those kinds of jobs one takes on the road to something bigger. For instance, Maria Alvarez is a recent graduate of Swarthmore College. In 2002, she led the school's knitting group. She recalled how *The Philadelphia Inquirer* wrote about the club back then as part of the "knitting fad."[11]

"Apparently it's still a fad," she said dryly as she whizzed through a row of stockinette stitch, never looking down at her needles during conversation. Alvarez and Kaufman are both frustrated that the media calls knitting a trend. Both women have been knitting since childhood.

"Knitting has been around for a long time," Kaufman said. Alvarez noted that many knitters probably disagree with her group's stance on abortion. Groups exist that knit to fund pro-life organizations as well, she noted. I chose to meet with the pro-choice knitting club because their political stance defies the stereotypical view of knitters as a subculture.

Knitting is a craft that requires the left and right halves of the brain to cooperate. For this reason, it attracts all kinds of people. One personal revelation my research has produced is that scientists and mathematicians often enjoy knitting.

It is easy to mistakenly compartmentalize people into male and female roles, artistic and scientific roles, domestic and career roles. Knitters defy such classification. They are so often multitalented, living lives that include many roles, perhaps even paradoxical ones.

Alvarez makes a great example. She studied biochemistry for two years before she switched her major to history. "I'm a big science nerd," she says. But she also loves art and has studied painting. Her political and humanitarian concerns extend beyond the abortion issue, too.

At Swarthmore, the knitting club made an afghan, selling it to raise money to buy blankets for homeless people. Initially, their idea was to knit many afghans for the homeless, but they quickly realized that the plan was impractical. Knitting even one afghan would take a very long time. If each member made one square for an afghan, she could experiment with fancy stitches, and the final product would fetch a higher price.

Only a group of people with ample quantities of both logic and creativity would come up with such a successful idea. The club was able to raffle off the afghan, raising enough money to buy many blankets for a local homeless shelter.

Kaufman offers another view of how art and science inspire and aid the knitter. When a course on topology sparked her imagination, she knitted an approximation of a Klein bottle—a theoretical shape whose inside and outside are composed of the same surface.

Knitters for Choice is just one of many knitting circles devoted to supporting a cause. Churches have long been home to knitting ministries. Often, church groups knit garments to benefit the needy, to comfort the sick, or even to celebrate an occasion like the birth of a child.

One popular source of inspiration for church knitting circles is the Prayer Shawl Ministry, the 1998 brainchild of Janet Brislow and Victoria Galo. The women developed a pattern for a shawl to be given to people as a comfort during times of grief, stress, illness, or change. Knitters are encouraged to pray for the recipient as they make the shawl. The ministry's Web site, http://www.shawlministry.com/, also features a list of shawl requests that church groups may fulfill, variations on the pattern, and stories submitted by both makers and recipients of shawls.

Laura Sponseller formed a knitting circle at Yale University's Battell Chapel. Sponseller was a student at Yale Divinity School and interned at the chapel during her final year at the school, just before heading off to finish studies for a medical degree. Members of her knitting circle included fellow students as well as New Haven residents who attend Battell.

The group knits scarves for homeless people in New Haven. They also draw inspiration from the Prayer Shawl Ministry, using their patterns and responding to a few pleas for shawls from groups that posted on the ministry's Web site. Other shawls were donated to people located through club members' own contacts. For instance, Hartford Hospital has a ministry for dying patients and their families. A couple of other people in need were identified individually.

"One thing that's neat is that people started putting knitted items in the offering plate at church," Sponseller said.[12] At the beginning of the fall 2005 school semester, the group attracted lots of undergraduates—mainly freshmen. "Especially for some of the freshmen, at the beginning of the semester before they knew people, it was a place for them to gather," Sponseller said. The circle pulled together expert knitters and novices. "I taught a lot of people to knit," Sponseller said.

Knitting for premature babies is the mission of Stitches of Love, founded at Providence Presbyterian Church in Quakertown, Pennsylvania. Since 2003, knitters have been donating afghans, hats, and even burial clothing and buntings for stillborn babies and those who die shortly after birth. In 2005, the knitters also started knitting dolls that police use to comfort children at a crime scene or to sensitively investigate suspected cases of child abuse. Knitters gather at area churches, and teenagers, shut-in adults, nursing home residents, and hospital staff also donate knitted items. Retailers and yarn manufacturers donate all the group's raw materials, and members will teach anyone to knit, crochet, or embroider.

While churches and nursing homes have long been knitting strongholds, ever more knitting circles are turning up in unlikely places. Former *Philadelphia Inquirer* columnist Lucia Herndon wrote about how social worker Kathy Duffy taught women to knit at Interim House, a residence for women with drug and alcohol addictions. Herndon's column prompted a flood of donations to the facility, including yarns, needles, and even a $500 check.[13]

"I was not surprised by the response," Herndon wrote in a later column. "I don't think I've met too many knitters who weren't kind and generous." Herndon also wrote about how The Wellness Community of Philadelphia, a support and information center for people with cancer, started a knitting circle in 2001.[14]

She publicized a 2003 knit-in that city officials organized in affiliation with an annual drive to collect warm garments for children, the Women Making a Difference Warmth in Winter Holiday Drive. Knitters gathered at a caucus room in Philadelphia's City Hall to make mittens, hats, and scarves. The city-sponsored knit-in takes place annually in Philadelphia as of 2006.

Teacher Debbie Bakan taught elementary school students to knit at Plymouth Meeting Friends School. She told Herndon that knitting helps children develop motor control, calms down "wiggly" kids, and can be used to improve math skills. Bakan even noticed her students' handwriting became better after they learned to knit. Knitting also provided an opportunity for the kids to perform community service. They made stuffed toys and blanket squares that adults would sew into blankets to be used in homeless shelters.

Charitable knitting is flourishing, and I can only scratch the surface here by naming some of the groups I know about. A major charitable knitting organization is Afghans for Afghans, which sends hand-knitted and crocheted blankets and garments to the impoverished people of Afghanistan. The group has been active since September 2001, and since then, it has shipped more than 30,000 blankets, sweaters, hats, mittens, gloves, and scarves to people in Heret, Jalalabad, and Kabul. The Agape Foundation funds the nonprofit, and volunteers make the items and distribute the gifts.[15]

The Dulaan Project, based in Flagstaff, Arizona, aims to provide warm clothing for people in one of the coldest regions in the world, Mongolia. The Mongolian word, "dulaan," means "warm" in English. According to the project's organizers, winter temperatures in Mongolia's capital city of Ulanbaatar rarely exceed freezing, and can sink to –40 degrees

Farenheit at night. The Dulaan Project is a cooperative effort of Flagstaff International Relief Effort (FIRE), Mossy Cottage Knits, and the Kunzang Palyul Choling (KPC) Buddhist community of Sedona.[16]

A relatively new kind of knitting circle is burgeoning. It consists of members who may never meet in person. As we shall see in the following chapter, the Internet provides a venue for total strangers to meet virtually and provide each other with nearly all the same benefits they would gain from belonging to an actual knitting circle. And, because it can be difficult to identify other knitters in the real world, knitters often use the Internet to draw members to real knitting circles in a town, city, or region. In fact, the Internet was the main conduit through which Debbie Stoller's Stitch 'N Bitch club trend got its footing.

8

KNITTING INTO THE ETHER: HOW THE INTERNET NOURISHED THE KNITTING TREND

Young knitters are tremendous users of the Internet. It would be difficult to overstate the influence the Internet has on the popularity of knitting. A Google search on the word "knitting," executed as I wrote this chapter in August 2006, generated about 38.4 million hits.

A nonknitter might find it odd that many practitioners of this ancient handicraft use high technology to share stories and images of their projects, to locate rare yarns and supplies, or to snag free patterns. Odder still is the notion of a virtual knitting circle, but that's what the Internet provides for many people, particularly those isolated from other knitters by geography or busy schedules that limit other means of socializing.

Internet resources for knitters are numerous. They include online stores, free knitting magazines, Web sites for guilds, clubs, and associations, and an abundance of blogs, which are online personal journals. Of all these destinations, blogs are the most interesting to this author, because web logging is so suited to the knitter's needs and habits. Another reason I'll give blogs special consideration is that, just as political bloggers have affected how professional outlets cover the news, knitting bloggers are predicting and even dictating the market for knitting books.

The number of knitting blogs grows constantly, and counting them all proves near impossible because none of the resources for blog statistics tracks all blogs. The leading tracker of blogs, Technorati, tracked 27.2 million blogs as of February 2006. Knitting blogs probably number several thousand, representing a small segment of the blogosphere. But the small world of knitting bloggers is very busy, very incestuous, and very powerful in terms of how it can affect the larger knitting market. Technorati has remarked on these niche bloggers and their influence.

Technorati writer Dave Sifry cited the most popular knitting blog, Yarn Harlot, in a comprehensive analysis of blog growth called "State of the Blogosphere."[1]

Though it's not among the A-List of Technorati's Top 100 blogs, Yarn Harlot is one of about 155,000 blogs that enjoy a large audience within the niche they address. These Magic Middle blogs are among the most interesting and influential in the blogosphere, according to Sifry.

"(Blogs) like Chocolate and Zucchini on food, Wi-fi Net News on Wireless networking, TechCrunch on Internet Companies, Blogging Baby on parenting, Yarn Harlot on knitting, or Stereogum on music— these are blogs that are interesting, topical, and influential, and in some cases are radically changing the economics of trade publishing," Sifry wrote.

YARN HARLOT: A STUDY IN BLOG POWER

Trackers like Technorati gauge the popularity of a blog based on the number of other Web sites that link to it. Links into a blog indicate that other bloggers or webmasters think the blog is important. Sifry defined The Magic Middle as blogs that have 20 to 1,000 other Web sites linking to them. In actuality, more than 5,000 sites link to Yarn Harlot, and the blog falls just outside Technorati's Top 100 on most days. As these pages were written, the blog ranked between 130 and 150.

Yarn Harlot is the Web site of Toronto-based knitter and author Stephanie Pearl-McPhee, a self-described Erma Bombeck of knitting humor. Pearl-McPhee has published three books on knitting since 2005: *At Knit's End: Meditations for Women Who Knit Too Much*, *The Yarn Harlot: The Secret Life of a Knitter*, and most recently, *Knitting Rules: The Yarn Harlot's Bag of Tricks*.

The Yarn Harlot is a rock star among knitters. When Yarn Harlot goes on tour, knitters bombard yarn stores and sometimes even pack by the hundreds into hotel convention halls. Fellow knitting bloggers will write on their blogs about meeting Pearl-McPhee. For her part, Pearl-McPhee thrills fans by photographing them with a half-done sock, cast onto double-pointed needles, which she carries during her travels. Later, the Harlot posts these photos on her blog.

Pearl-McPhee's fans seek their own brush with celebrity through contact with Yarn Harlot. Pearl-McPhee is known to respond to bloggers' comments, to post many links to her readers' blogs, and to publish their faces there, too.

Pearl-McPhee is more famous for her humor than her knitting acumen, though she is a talented and prolific knitter. Another well-known knitting blogger, Kay Gardiner of Mason-Dixon Knitting, pointed to two distinct kinds of knitting blog: the kind that focuses squarely knitting projects, sharing technique, photos, and patterns; and the sort that is personality-driven, in which the blogger tells stories about her life in general, which often happens to involve knitting. Some of the most successful knitting blogs fall into the second category, and Yarn Harlot is among them.

"It's just like a really good soap opera," Gardiner said of Pearl-McPhee's blog. "There's all the characters, and you need to know what happens next."

The name "Yarn Harlot" derives from a back-page essay Pearl-McPhee wrote for *Interweave Knits* magazine. The essay was about second sock syndrome. That's when a knitter, having finished the first in a pair of socks, dreads doing the exact same knitting all over again to make the second sock and, as Pearl-McPhee aptly puts it, "hears the siren call of twenty-nine other projects."

"It was about my struggle to stay with one project," Pearl-McPhee said in an interview with this author. "I lost the battle. I said I'd rather look for a cross-dressing pirate than knit the second pink lace sock. I can't be monogamous to any one project. I'm just a yarn harlot."

People go to Pearl-McPhee's blog for a laugh and a sense of community. She is apt to describe mundane daily challenges hilariously: the alarm clock that went off too early, the hole that contractors left in the side of her house, the war with birds who ate all the sour cherries from her tree, just as she figured out what to bake with them.

When asked if she knows how many readers she has, she declines to comment. "I usually don't tell people," she said. "It's part of my Zen personality that says it's wrong to compete. I don't want to be that girl in the playground saying, 'I have five friends, and you only have three friends.'"

Pearl-McPhee said she also tries to avoid looking at blog statistics too often. "It's not healthy," she said. "To count your friends every day leads to editing yourself, thinking about what you say. Sometimes I worry this blogging thing is turning us into Pavlovian dogs. I try not to let myself get like that."

Nonetheless, it became clear in winter of 2006 that Yarn Harlot was a force to be reckoned with. During the 2006 Winter Olympics, Pearl-McPhee started a phenomenon when she called upon knitters worldwide to take part in their own competition: The Knitting Olympics. She urged knitters to choose their own project—something that would challenge them—and complete it within the time span of the actual Olympic Games, that is, sixteen days. Projects were to be cast onto the needles during opening ceremonies and bound off before the Olympic flame was extinguished. Self-reporting "champions," that is, those who finished their projects on time, were awarded a virtual gold medal, which was an electronic button they could display on their own blogs. They also qualified for a raffle Pearl-McPhee conducted using prizes donated by various yarn and knitting supply sources.

These virtual games attracted a remarkable amount of attention. All told, 4,071 knitting "athletes" officially entered the games by listing what they would knit on Pearl-McPhee's blog. That's nearly twice the number of athletes in the actual Olympic Games. Their projects included everything from simple scarves to complicated Fair Isle sweaters. Major news outlets, including *The Oregonian* of Portland, British Broadcasting Company, and numerous Canadian television networks, covered The Knitting Olympics.

In my interview with Pearl-McPhee, I tried to tease out of her what she thinks are the reasons for her success in the unlikely niche of humor writing about knitting.[2] Pearl-McPhee says she has always loved to write but got a sense she might be able to sell her knack with words after joining an e-mail listserv for knitters called Knit List, which includes about 10,000 participants. She wrote one or two letters a month through Knit List, and fellow members started commenting on how funny she was.

In the end, necessity led Pearl-McPhee to test her mettle as a knitting humorist. Both she and her husband were out of work for several months when the SARS pandemic arrived in Canada.

Pearl-McPhee works as a doula and lactation consultant; she guides women through childbirth and breastfeeding. When SARS was discovered in Canadian hospitals, the government contained the pandemic by allowing only essential workers to enter hospitals, meaning those who were required to keep patients alive. Doulas were kept out, and the company that Pearl-McPhee worked for was ruined.

Meanwhile, her husband's work as a record producer and sound mixer for film also dried up. Much of his work involved American films, and the United States issued a travel advisory prohibiting flights to and from Canada for several months, Pearl-McPhee said.

Pearl-McPhee, her husband, and their two daughters ripped through their savings quickly, and panic set in. "I lay in bed one night thinking about money," Pearl-McPhee said. She asked herself, "What am I good at? I'm good at writing. I'm good at knitting." "Then I thought, 'Shit. This is never going to work. What am I going to do, write about knitting?'"

At that point, she had published some essays in a series of anthologies called *Knit Lit*. That gave her some hope. Pearl-McPhee contacted an agent to pitch her idea: she wanted to write a funny book about knitting.

"I wrote up a book proposal, and everybody turned it down," she said. "They said people wouldn't buy funny books about knitting." But one company, Storey Publishing, said they would be interested in writing a popcorn book—a spoof on the self-help titles of the eighties like *Meditations for Women Who Love Too Much*. Pearl-McPhee balked at their proposed title: *At Knit's End: Meditations for Women Who Knit Too Much*. She wanted to address her book to people, not just women, because men knit, too. But the publisher was firm about keeping their chosen title, and, as Pearl-McPhee puts it, "I would have eaten worms for money."

Her compendium of tongue-in-cheek advice for obsessive knitters was a top seller. Pearl-McPhee said she didn't start up her blog until after she'd gotten a book deal.

"I had been reading blogs and having a really good time," she said. A friend with computer savvy noticed her interest and built her blog as a Christmas gift. "I just loved it," Pearl-McPhee said. Pearl-McPhee insists that she never intended for her blog to be a tool for selling her books.

"I decided really early that my blog would be my living room, not a marketing force," she said, noting that she rarely mentions her books in her blog entries. "I feel that's like trying to sell Amway to someone when you invite them over for dinner. It's not very polite."

She believes that the blog is a nearly perfect venue for knitters. "It's the world's fastest, most efficient show-and-tell," Pearl-McPhee said. She said photos are what most blog visitors visit her site to see. "On a slow day, I can just post a picture and say, 'Here's how it's going.' It's the same as going to a knitting guild where somebody holds up their sweater."

Pearl-McPhee wouldn't name her favorite blogs, but she did speculate on what makes certain blogs popular. "Popular blogs aren't even good blogs," she said. "Some of these people can't write their way out of a paper bag." The biggest secret to a blogger's popularity, she said, is frequent posts. "People love predictability," Pearl-McPhee said. "You become a habit for them."

Still not naming names, Pearl-McPhee pointed out that there's one knitting blogger who enjoys great popularity despite a lack of writing talent. What that blogger gives to readers is lots of knitting expertise and regular posts. And these are traits knitters seem to value most in a blogger. "She's a good knitter, and she knits a lot," Pearl-McPhee said. "It proves out the theory that it's about the knitting."

Yarn Harlot takes special pride in the fact that her blog doesn't only appeal to knitters, though. Some people read the blog just for the humor. She's not really famous, she knows. "I can still go to the grocery store unaccosted," she said. "I'm only famous in yarn shops."

And yet, she is having a notable influence on book publishing. The success of Pearl-McPhee's books appears to have affected the proliferation of knitting authors on the whole and, particularly, those with knitting blogs.

Several other bloggers whose sites are linked to Pearl-McPhee's through the Knitting Bloggers net ring have published books in 2006. The most popular of these blogs are Mason-Dixon Knitting and Wendy Knits.

Mason-Dixon Knitting is the shared blog of Kay Gardiner and Ann Shayne. They are two knitters who became online friends years before they ever met in person. Gardiner lives in Manhattan, while Shayne lives in Nashville. In 2006, Gardiner and Shayne published a knitting book, *Mason-Dixon Knitting: The Curious Knitter's Guide*.[3] Wendy Knits is the blog of Wendy Johnson, a knitter since age four, who fans admire particularly for her expertise and ability to clearly explain even tough techniques. Johnson's blog is largely a catalog of her many, many knitting projects, with detailed explanations. She also posts numerous photos of Lucy, her cat, fulfilling a somewhat accurate stereotype about knitters and their love for the feline species. Johnson is one of the earliest knit bloggers; her first Web site that logged knitting projects was published in 1996. In April 2006 she published *Wendy Knits: My Never-Ending Adventures in Yarn*.[4]

I interviewed Kay Gardiner of Mason-Dixon Knitting because the story of how that blog evolved reveals much about how meaningful knitting and blogging have become to the lives of many people who practice both activities.

MASON-DIXON KNITTING: THE VIRTUAL TIES THAT BIND

Kay Gardiner is glad to know that someone is analyzing the current knitting trend. Though young knitters have garnered much press enthusiasm in recent years—hardly a major media outlet exists that has *not* published something about the craze—articles tend to portray the knitting revival as something quaint and trivial. Many knitters say they resent that diminution of an activity that, in frequent instances, has reshaped lives.

Gardiner's own life is completely refashioned since 2001, when she left her career of a dozen years as an assistant U.S. attorney in Manhattan and devoted herself to raising her children. As a mother, she spent a lot of time accompanying her kids to their various appointments and waiting for them. She had been knitting for years, but after quitting her job, she said, "I was starting to get into (knitting) almost in a way that was kind of icky."

The first time she questioned the normalcy of her knitting obsession was around the time she signed up to become a member of Rowan International, an online club for knitters sponsored by the Rowan yarn company in the United Kingdom. Rowan sells classic, high-end yarns in subdued colors that reflect a decidedly English aesthetic. Fans of the brand and, specifically, those who pay to subscribe to Rowan International, are called Rowanettes among cognoscenti.

One of the most coveted features of Rowan International membership before the dawn of knitting blogs was an online bulletin board, which allowed Rowanettes across the globe to communicate. It was here, and on other e-mail list servers that predated most blogs, that knitters like Gardiner first discovered the usefulness of the Internet in informing their craft.

Beyond providing knitting advice, though, the electronic bulletin board allowed many knitters to make new friends in distant places. Gardiner and Shayne first made contact serendipitously in 2001 through the Rowan board, when both women were knitting the same sweater at the same time, and both encountered the same problem, Gardiner said.

The sweater featured a sleeve with lots of stitch details. Once all the details had been knitted, the sleeves were too long, almost twice as long as a person's arms, according to Gardiner.

When Gardiner learned that Shayne was knitting her sweater in navy and green, she imagined a woman more conservative and, she presumed, much older than herself. In fact, Shayne is younger than Gardiner.

The two knitters didn't e-mail each other directly until about a year later. That was when Gardiner stopped checking into the Rowan bulletin board for a while because her daughter was ill and other challenges in her family life were keeping her busy, she said. Shayne took notice of Gardiner's absence and commented on it to fellow Rowanettes. She obtained Gardiner's e-mail address, and the two women started corresponding directly. Gardiner said her online friendship with Shayne essentially replaced her interest in the Rowan chat board. She stopped visiting it.

E-mails between Gardiner, in New York City, and Shayne, in Nashville, Tennessee, had a different tone altogether than the comments each had posted on the Rowan board, Gardiner said.

"From very early on, we would write to each other like we were very good friends," Gardiner said. The women shared news of big changes in their lives regarding career and family.

"We were both lonely, even with lots of friends," Gardiner said. Discussions had never been so frank or intimate on the electronic bulletin board, she said. "When you're in a chat room or blog, it's like being in someone's living room," Gardiner said. "You need to be polite."

In July 2003 the e-mailing friends decided to make their correspondence public by publishing a blog together. After struggling unsuccessfully to use the free blogging tool Blogger, they decided to hire another blogger named Becky Delgado, who writes the blog Fluffa! to host Mason-Dixon Knitting. Delgado hosts several knitting blogs through her service, Pretty Posies. Then Gardiner and Shayne signed up with the Knitting Bloggers NetRing and were among the first 300 bloggers registered there.

Since that time, Mason-Dixon Knitting has become one of the most popular knitting blogs on the Internet. Even so, Gardiner and Shayne didn't meet in person until September 2004, after they had a book deal. Gardiner said she and Shayne were both busy and didn't have any reason to visit each other's hometowns.

They had contemplated writing a book together for a while, but it took a literary agent's interest in their blog to give them the gumption to follow through, Gardiner said. Both women enjoyed writing and felt comfortable doing it. Shayne had worked in publishing, and Gardiner wrote a lot of briefs as a lawyer. Out of the blue, an agent contacted them by e-mail about writing a book. That agent was pitching an idea that didn't interest the women, but the inquiry gave them courage. They were able to find a New York agent, write a book proposal, and have the proposal accepted at one of their top choices of publishers.

Gardiner said her perspective on knitters' use of the Internet has changed since she first signed up to be a Rowanette. Back then, she thought knitting blogs were a little nutty, she said. Now she sees blogging as an important vehicle for the knitting community. "It's a subculture within a subculture," Gardiner said. "It's one of the most fascinating things I've ever encountered in my life."

Only a handful of knitting bloggers cinch book deals. Many others blog away in relative anonymity. Their goals as bloggers are most often friendship with people who share their interests, access to advice and encouragement, and the creation of a knitting history.

YARN-A-GO-GO

Rachael Herron never intended to write a knitting blog. She is a 911 dispatcher in Oakland, California. She is in her thirties, and she has an M.F.A. in writing from Mills College. She launched a web journal called Yarn-A-Go-Go in 2001 because she wanted to jump-start her writing life. Herron has been a regular knitter since she learned the skill at age five, and so, naturally, she found herself writing about the craft.

"I thought no one would ever, ever, ever look at it," she said of her blog. As of September 2006, about 120,000 people view Herron's blog each month. As more and more Internet traffic filtered and linked to her site, Herron found herself insisting to knitting readers, "It's not a knitting blog! It's more than that."

Her blog, she said, is a spin-off of hardcore knitting blogs that focus strictly on knitting photos, patterns, technique, and advice. On Yarn-A-Go-Go, Herron addresses knitting, yes, but only to the extent that it fits into the rest of her life. On any given day, viewers may read posts about knitting, but they might also encounter entries about Herron's travel to Italy or her relationship with her life partner Lala Hulse, who she met on the Internet.

Herron admits, "Knitting and fiber is the biggest obsession I have," and she says the greatest surprise and gift her blog has provided is a huge network of knitting friends around the world.

"I have amazing readers, and a lot of them are an amazing circle of knitting women who are the smartest, the funniest—and they know everything," Herron said. "If I want to know a good restaurant to go to in Taipei, they can recommend one. So many of them are my good, true friends." Like many knitting bloggers, Herron sometimes seeks to get to know certain bloggers better by meeting them in person.

"I've done yarn crawls," she said, where groups of knitting bloggers gather to check out an area's yarn shops together. She will also occasionally send out a call on her blog to Bay Area knitters to get together at a particular café to knit. Later, knitters who attended such a gathering might post blog entries about the meet-up, including photos and links to the blogs of knitters they met in person. Remember that each link a blogger posts enhances the prominence and credibility of the linked-to blogger and is likely to increase traffic to that blog. At the events Herron organizes, she said, friendships often form that transcend the more superficial nature of blog connections. She recalled a recent gathering of knitters where the conversation was so intense that everyone attending forgot to take photos to post on their blogs. "It went beyond remembering to blog," she said.

Sometimes bloggers will form special correspondences with people they meet through their blogs and will travel far afield to meet in person. Herron has crossed the country to meet bloggers on the East Coast. She said that for many bloggers, the first in-person visit to a fellow blogger is fraught with anxiety. Herron's first such visit was to a blogger and university professor in Philadelphia.

"I was so nervous," Herron said. "It felt like a blind date. I didn't know if she would like me. The other thing is I thought, 'You know so much about me, but you know so little about me.'"

Bloggers frequently describe the odd experience of being recognized at knitting, yarn, or fiber-related events by people who read their blogs. The stranger may recognize them from blog photos, and they may comment on personal aspects of a blogger's life that the blogger had forgotten writing about.

Gardiner, of Mason-Dixon Knitting, remarked on how her husband found it slightly eerie that a reader recognized their daughter at one festival. Gardiner was less alarmed, saying she has come to be very trusting of the knitting community. "She knows who my daughter is," Gardiner said of the woman at the festival. "She's a knitter; what's she going to do? Knit her something?"

Pearl-McPhee remembered feeling startled when, at a book signing, a reader mentioned her living room was painted in the same color. "I thought, 'How do you know what color my living room is?' and then I remembered I'd blogged about it," she said.

More often than not, Herron said, she is pleasantly startled by the assumed intimacy and the immediate trust among knitting bloggers. She recounted one visit to a lifelong resident of the island of Nantucket in Massachusetts. Her host was a fan of her blog whom she had never met in person. Herron met the fan at a pub during the woman's lunch break from work.

"She gave us her car for the day and then took us home and made us dinner," Herron recalled. That night, Herron stayed at the woman's farmhouse, which had been in her family for nine generations.

Though Herron is not one of those rare knitters whose blog lands them a book deal, Yarn-A-Go-Go has changed her life, she said. "It has kind of influenced everything in a big way," she said. "It's as if I have this audience I never anticipated, and, not only an audience, but a group I feel I owe something to. I want to make them proud of me."

FINDING THEIR NICHE: NET RINGS AND KNIT-ALONGS

Online knitters sometimes organize themselves into virtual societies with common interests. Often bloggers subscribe to net rings or web rings, which are communities of Web sites on a particular topic that are linked. Visitors to a site within the net ring can use a navigational tool to browse through all the sites in the ring. Subscribers to the ring typically must obey rules on keeping content focused to the ring's subject matter and posting with a certain level of frequency. Bloggers can belong to more than one net ring.

The largest net ring for knitters is the Knitting Bloggers. This ring, established in 2002, had about 1,000 active members by fall 2006, with more than 100 bloggers waiting to join. Members include the big three—Yarn Harlot, Wendy Knits, and Mason-Dixon Knitting—and other blogs in the ring enjoy high profiles, as well.

Belonging to a major net ring like Knitting Bloggers is a way to increase the likelihood of traffic to a blog, but now that the ring is so large, newer bloggers are finding it harder to attract an audience.

At the start of the knitting blog trend, around 2002, Gardiner recalls that net ring members would often visit every blog on the ring. Today, the glut of blogs makes visiting each one nearly impossible.

Herron, of Yarn-A-Go-Go, said the knitting blog community, once such a haven for people who might have felt outcast by larger society, seems to be developing cliques. When new bloggers consult Herron about how to increase their traffic, she said, she tells them not to look for a flood of comments or to obsess over traffic statistics. Instead, they should reach out to blogs that began around the same time that theirs did. "I tell them, that's going to be your base in years to come," she said.

Some net rings for knitters cater to even smaller niches than just knitting. For instance, more than 440 knitting bloggers who own cats form the Knitting Kitty net ring. Men Who Knit, a ring that joins male knitters (though it does not exclude women) has 100 members and is closed, with twenty members waiting to enter the ring.

Some rings narrow membership by geography, like the California Knit Ring Bloggers with about 300 members, New England Knitters with about 200 knitters, or Southern Knit Bloggers with about 300 members.

Other knitting net rings focus on a particular type of knitting, such as lace knitting, sock knitting, or Aran knitting. Perhaps the most exclusive net ring is one devoted to knitting women named Wendy.[5] Founded in May 2005, the Knitting Wendys net ring includes twenty active members and nine prospective members as of September 2006. This ring no doubt evolved because Wendy Johnson of Wendy Knits is among the first and best known of all knitting bloggers, and so, other knitters named Wendy usually have to explain that they are not she.

Still more net rings cast a wider net, inviting knitters and crocheters or all fiber artists. For instance, Random Acts of Kindness is a fiber arts ring whose members must agree to send gifts or kind words to others within the ring, particularly when their blogging indicates they are going through hard times. Queer Knits, formed in November 2002, is a ring devoted to gay and lesbian knitters and crocheters with 188 members and fifty waiting for membership.

GAY AND LESBIAN KNITTERS

A notable number of gay and lesbian knitters formed blogs early in the knitting blog trend. Herron is among this group. She said many of her peers have struggled to isolate why gays and lesbians were so apt to join the knitting revival. During our interview, our musings led us to a possible connection.

I mentioned to Herron my truly enlightening encounter with New Haven knitter Lauren Lax. Lax is not gay, nor is she obviously non-conformist. She is working on doctoral degree in business at Yale and was adamant about keeping her knitting blog a secret. She feared her father would discover the blog and disapprove of her knitting obsession. At the same time, on the very evening we met, Lax invited me into her home and literally opened up her closets, showing me hordes of yarn, piles of gorgeous sweaters, and rows of knitting books and patterns. Lax came out of the closet to me. And here, I am "outing" her as a knitter to the world. I pray she will forgive my indiscretion; I could not keep her secret. For one thing, I do not believe she wanted to keep the secret herself. If she wished to stay closeted, why did she invite me in? Beyond this, her knitting, her secret life that is such a rich, beautiful, and generous world, is just too vivid a glimpse into the heart of this subculture. Asking me to help cloister this gift is too much to ask. I will give a fuller account of my meeting with Lax later in this chapter.

The knitting underground, if you will, is much like the alternative universe of gays and lesbians. Both worlds are still so separate from mainstream American life that they almost exist on another plane. Some people choose to ignore their existence. Other people mock, disparage, or otherwise diminish the importance of their passion.

The difference between these two subcultures is that gays and lesbians are susceptible to a far greater and more dangerous contempt from society than knitters will ever encounter. A person who knits in public risks being labeled a geek, a granny, or at the worst, someone less important because he or she is displaying what society sees as feminine behavior.

An openly gay person risks and often suffers rejection by the people he loves most and hostility from the general public. In a very real way, an openly gay person risks violence and even death by revealing his true nature.

Perhaps a comfort with marginalization is the main reason why gays and lesbians have been so willing to identify with the subculture of knitters. Herron cinched it:

"You're already in the minority and you have everybody looking at you funny," Herron said. "In that sense, you don't care if something you do is a little bit nutty. It's like those young gay boys who sew their own prom dress and wear it to the prom. Nothing anyone says about them is going to make them feel any worse."

Herron also equated the first few years after a gay person comes out to a knitter's introduction to the world of knitters on the Internet.

"The next few years (after coming out as homosexual) are the most exciting," she said. "It's like you're an adolescent all over again, except this time you get to date the gender you want to date. Knitters who find other knitters, and when they find this blog world out there, there's that level of excitement that's huge."

Kay Gardiner described the same kind of enthusiasm when she talked about young, new knitters in general. "I'm like their den mother because they're so very young," Gardiner said of the young women who knit with her in New York. "Some of them go into it at an incredible depth. When they discover something (a new aspect of knitting), it's like they invented it. . . . They go into it with all their might."

Gardiner said she has seen young knitters plunge into love with socks, spinning, felting, and lace. These young knitters may, for instance, invest thousands of dollars in supplies, spend hundreds of hours on their new interest, and quickly become expert at their chosen specialty.

KNIT-ALONGS, EXCHANGES, AND SECRET PALS

Beyond net rings, other devices also allow knitters to get to know each other better. One popular device is the knit-along, which unites knitters who are all working individually on the same project. Members of the knit-along communicate through a Web site, where they post photos of their works in progress (known in knitting shorthand as WIPs) or their finished objects (also called FOs). They will also ask for and give advice and links to sites that provide ideal yarns, tools, or notions for the project.

The number and popularity of knit-alongs devoted to a particular project or type of knitting can suggest trends in the overall knitting community. In the past two years, a few trends were evident. Knitters turned their attention en masse to felting (napping knitted yarn to form a surface like felt), sock knitting, lace knitting, dyeing, and spinning.

Another way in which knitters collaborate online is by joining exchanges, such as Secret Pal. Knitting bloggers sign on to the Secret Pal Web site to give and receive anonymous gifts to each other. Care packages often contain yarn, knitted items, tools, and fun gadgets for knitting, patterns, or items to enhance the knitting experience, such as teas, cocoas, cookies, or chocolate. Sometimes during exchanges, a gift giver will include items that cater to the tastes and needs of the recipient, which the giver has gleaned by reading the recipient's blog.

"All these exchanges and a lot of activities, I think, are to make these relationships more real," Gardiner said.

CLAPOTIS: A CRAZE WITHIN A CRAZE

One pattern that captured the attention of the online knitting masses is Clapotis, which was published in the fall 2004 issue of the online knitting magazine, *Knitty*. Clapotis is a scarf knitted on the bias in variegated color yarn so that the garment sports diagonal stripes. Then stitches are dropped at regular intervals to create vertical ladders of yarn that add textural interest and a pleasant drape. The end result is a complex visual effect that is deceptively simple to execute.

Check out this listing of Clapotis references on the blog Knitting In Public: http://www.gusset.net/kip/archives/000509.html. Particularly amusing is one knitter's homage to both the scarf and the poet Wallace Stevens in her own poem, *Thirteen Ways of Looking at Clapotis*, on the blog http://dogsstealyarn.com/.

Kate Gilbert, Clapotis' designer, has been a knitter since her teen years.[6] "I kept seeing things here and there about knitting," Gilbert said. "I saw an old movie on T.V., and Cary Grant was knitting. I later found out that my grandmother was a big knitter. She died when my father was sixteen." When Gilbert took up knitting, she said, "My mother was convinced that it was because of Grandma Ruth."

Gilbert grew up in New York but moved to Paris for four years, where she lived with her French husband, Fred. The couple recently moved to Montreal with their baby daughter. But it was in France that Gilbert was inspired by women's avid use of scarves to design Clapotis, she said.

"I really wanted to make something simple," Gilbert said. "I was sitting in the Metro messing around with some different stitch patterns and said, 'What if I dropped this stitch? What if I did it crooked instead of straight?'"

When she settled on a pattern, she e-mailed *Knitty* editor Amy Singer to pitch her idea. Singer agreed to publish Clapotis and supplied the yarn, a luxurious silk-wool blend by Lorna's Laces called Lion and Lamb.

Gilbert never thought her pattern would become so popular. It is probably the most popular free knitting pattern in the world. "I didn't think anybody would like it," Gilbert said. "I figured they would want something flashier."

In fact, as she watched message boards for knitters shortly after the fall 2004 issue of *Knitty* was published, she saw little buzz about Clapotis, she said. The pattern's popularity would increase later. "I guess it just sort of caught on," Gilbert said. "People started e-mailing me telling me they really liked it." Soon she was flooded with questions about the pattern and images knitters sent her of their own finished versions of the scarf.

Gilbert's pattern may be famous in the online world of young knitters, but she remains anonymous. For one thing, Gilbert was living in Paris when the pattern was published and all through the online buzz about Clapotis.

"I missed it completely," she said. "Knitting was not the big deal in France that it is here," Gilbert said. "It's just starting to get big there now."

Another reason Gilbert wasn't spotted by knitters on the streets is that they usually didn't recognize her from her photo posted at the end of the Clapotis pattern on *Knitty*, she said. When she introduced herself as the scarf's designer, knitters would often confess they confused her with the scarf's model, Gilbert's friend, Émilie Vandenameele.

Gilbert said that, ironically, she missed being part of the knitting craze as it passed through each place she had lived in recent years. When her home was New York City, she worked as a web and magazine page designer for *BUST*, the feminist magazine published by knitting diva Debbie Stoller. Gilbert worked closely with Stoller and belonged to New York Stitch 'N Bitch, but the club wasn't all that popular when she belonged to it, she said. "Sometimes it would just be me and Debbie at her house," she said.

It seemed to Gilbert that as soon as she left for France, the knitting craze exploded. The name "Clapotis" was Gilbert's second choice, she said. She wanted to name the scarf "Ripple," but *Knitty* had already published a sock pattern called "Broadripple."

Singer wanted the scarf to have a French name. She suggested several French words that might suit the scarf, and Clapotis was among them. "I made Fred figure it out," Gilbert said about the name. "It means something like, 'little ripples in waves.'"

The name worked because it's a great description of how the columns of dropped stitches create a wavy drape in the scarf's silken knitted fabric. It turns out that most people don't wear their finished Clapotis scarves as Gilbert intended, she said.

"Everybody wears their Clapotis inside out," Gilbert said. "You're supposed to wear it with the reverse-stocking side out. I would always twist it when I put it on, and it would make waves. When you drop the stitches, they pop."

Then again, a few people have told Gilbert they like the scarf better the other way, and she accepts that. Gilbert continues to sell her patterns, but she doesn't knit for money anymore, because she found she could barely break even. She also designs patterns for the magazines *Interweave Knits* and *Knit Scene*.

The rage over Clapotis has died down somewhat, but Gilbert says she still receives e-mails about the pattern. A brief Internet search on the word clapotis quickly demonstrates the scarf's widespread appeal.

A Clapotis knit-along sponsored by Yahoo web group has 1,650 members. About 500 messages are posted to this site each month since it was established in 2005. Dozens of knitting bloggers have written about their experiences with Clapotis. Some bloggers have colloquially referred to Gilbert's scarf design as "The Clapper." Often young knitters will assume that other young knitters are familiar with the pattern.

Pearl-McPhee even made reference to Clapotis on her blog Yarn Harlot, railing against fans who implored her to knit the scarf.[7] "I will remain unmoved even if you write poetry about it," she wrote. "I will not knit it even if it is recommended to me by the Editor of Knitty." She, like Clapotis itself, is biased. "I will not knit it even if you call it 'The Clapper,' thus making it sound . . . more fun and funky than it already did. (As well as rather vaguely like a venereal disease.)"

BLOG CHARITY

Exchanges, also known as swaps, were the inspiration for Gardiner's idea to use knitting blogs for a charitable purpose. Mason-Dixon Knitting was among the first blogs to benefit a charity, but many others have since followed suit.

Mason-Dixon readers were asked to knit eight-by-eight-inch squares that would be made into blankets for the organization Afghans for Afghans, which provides warm woolen garments for poor villagers in Afghanistan. Bloggers and blog readers met in person during parties across the country where they sewed the squares together.

"We thought if we were lucky we would get forty to fifty squares," Gardiner said. "That's enough to make an afghan. We got over 2,000."

Readers wrote comments to Mason-Dixon Knitting requesting to host parties, so the project came to involve a lot of mailing. Each time Gardiner and Shayne sent out a bunch of squares to someone hosting a party, they would write posts about the endeavor.

Over time, charitable knitting, as well as just plain charity among knitting bloggers, has exploded. Yarn Harlot hosted an effort to raise money for Canadian Doctors Without Borders, also known in Canada as Medicins Sans Frontieres (MSF Canada). Pearl-McPhee set up Tricoteuses Sans Frontieres (Knitters Without Borders) in response to the December 2004 tsunami that killed 150,000 people in Southeast Asia.

Pearl-McPhee learned much about the devastation of the tsunami because her brother-in-law, Ben Chapman, is human resources director for MSF Canada. She told her readers about MSF's efforts to give medical aid and human rights to people in some of the poorest and most disenfranchised parts of the world, and she reminded readers of their relative wealth. She implored them to consider donating to MSF each time they got ready to buy something they didn't really need. She asked them to notify her of their donations so that she might keep a running tally on her blog. Pearl-McPhee said total donations from her readers have not been updated recently on her blog, but she knows they amount to well over $120,000.

On the blog, Now Norma Knits, a blogger named Norma encouraged fellow knitters to knit red scarves for children who have aged out of the foster care system and who head off to college. Once in school, the young adults have no foster families to live with during breaks. The Orphan Foundation of America distributes the scarves in care packages, and a new scarf-knitting campaign is in the works for 2007.

When fellow bloggers started commenting on Norma's generous efforts for OFA and for the Dulaan Project, which takes donated knitted items for poor people in Mongolia, here's what Norma had to say: "Anyhoo, it strikes me as totally uncharacteristic of me that I have unwittingly become such a big cheerleader for charity knitting. Because really, I am a Selfish Bitch [*sic*]."[8] Gardiner said this sort of generosity is one of the reasons that the knitting blog community is so attractive to her.

"There's a lot of things about this little community—it's not better than any group of people. There are people who are attention seekers. There are people who have some other agenda. But there are so many extraordinary people who would send an afghan square, or knit a red scarf."

Another remarkable demonstration of generosity took place on behalf of a longtime member of the knitting blog community. A knitter named Emma started her blog, Emma & Company, in November 2002. Emma is a prolific knitter and blogger living in England with her husband Allen, and son Oliver who suffers from cerebral palsy. Emma's blog generated a large following over the years, and she wrote often about the many exchanges of yarn and related gifts that she enjoyed with fellow knitting bloggers. In 2005, Emma made known her family's struggles to afford the best technology to help her then five-year-old son be as ambulatory and free as possible. The wheelchair the family hoped to buy cost the equivalent of about $20,000, according to Gardiner, who described the situation to me.

Knitting bloggers responded by urging Emma to set up an account to which they could donate money. In Northeast Ohio, a blogger named Barbara wrote this in a comment to Emma:

"Please believe me when I say the Internet knitblogging community is your neighborhood. Neighbors help each other when it's really needed. Let us extend a helping hand. I really hope you will set up the PayPal account."

Though she clearly felt awkward about doing so, Emma set up a PayPal account to allow her blogging friends around the world to contribute to Oliver's Fund, named for her son. Donations flooded the account, and many were made anonymously. Some knitting bloggers raised money creatively. Some of those with Internet businesses sold items and donated the profits to Oliver's Fund. Thomas Holm, whose blog is called Ravings from a Danish City at Night, knitted a lace shawl and auctioned it on eBay, donating the proceeds to Emma. Other bloggers have also knitted items to sell at auction for Oliver's benefit.

In the end, Emma was able to purchase a state-of-the-art electronic wheelchair, a chair lift, a specially equipped tricycle and a car seat for her son. A regional charity organization called the Variety Club agreed to match funds once Emma raised a certain amount on her own.

"Most of these people (who donated to Oliver's Fund) didn't even send her e-mails," said Gardiner, who befriended Emma online and has since visited her twice in the United Kingdom. "She was saying, 'There's money in my PayPal account, and I can't tell who it's from, to thank them.'"

New charity efforts by knitters are proliferating. In the United Kingdom, an online shop called I Knit (www.iknit.org.uk/knitariver.html) is organizing a project called Knit a River to benefit the organization Water Aid, which works for clean and safe water and toilets for poor people. I Knit is asking people to knit fifteen-by-fifteen centimeter blue squares that will be sewn together to form a knitted band resembling a river. They intend to use the piece as a kind of petition to raise awareness about their cause. The site notes that more than one billion people lack access to clean water, and more than two billion do not have sanitary conditions.

Word is also spreading via the Internet about an effort to, once again, knit socks for U.S. soldiers abroad. Socks For Soldiers (http://groups.yahoo.com/group/sockforsoldiers) is a group of knitters who send hand-knitted black socks to American soldiers in the Middle East. Kim Opperman of Mansfield, Ohio had been knitting socks for her son in the Air Force. She founded Socks for Soldiers when he told her he wished everyone in the military could have a pair of her hand-knitted socks. According to Opperman, many soldiers still say that military issue socks, made of synthetic fibers, wear out too quickly and sometimes cause blisters. The organization Keystone Soldiers ships the socks, which are sent to military personnel in care packages along with toiletries and treats. Socks for Soldiers has set a goal to gather 100,000 hand-knit socks. The group asks donors to contribute large, black, hand-knit socks in good quality, natural-fiber yarns with elasticity to prevent drooping. Donors are entered into random contests and giveaways of knitting supplies.

In an interesting turn of events, I learned about Socks for Soldiers through an e-mail that members of Knitters for Choice forwarded to me. Opperman noted in her missive, "We are a unique organization, as compared to the sock knitters of (World War II), in that because of the high technology age in which we live we have joined hands across the world for a common mission."

Opperman urged knitters to set aside their opinions about politics behind the war. "Our effort is a mission of love, where we are 'solely' focused on sending a clear message to our loved ones in Iraq: We might hate this war, but we love you and appreciate your service to this great country."

MORE ON WHY BLOGGING AND KNITTING CLICK

At this point I hope it is clear that the blog is a medium well suited to knitters' needs and interests. This fact may seem strange to someone who believes the stereotype that knitters are traditional and grandmotherly, or to someone who views knitting as a profoundly solitary act.

Much of this book works toward dispelling the grandma stereotype. It's also worth mentioning that grandmothers often defy their stereotype. My husband's fraternal grandmother, Helen Wills, in her mid-eighties and living in the rural Midwest, is supremely technologically savvy. She e-mails us regularly and surfs the Internet. An avid knitter for most of her life, Wills' church-based knitting ministry shares their needlecraft skills with inmates at an area prison.

Often younger knitters segregate themselves from older knitters, and that is their loss. If you are a young knitter, I urge you to make a concerted effort to meet an older knitter and pick his or her brain, and not just about knitting. As the subject of the knitting stereotype, you already know that stereotypes are dangerous. Befriend a senior citizen, and you may come to see how hazardous our stereotypes can be; so much—wisdom, history, and friendship—is forsaken when we ignore and discount the elderly. Enough digression—let us get back to blogs and why so many knitters use them.

SOMEONE WHO GETS IT

Blogging serves a lot of practical purposes for knitters. For one thing, keeping a journal about your knitting projects, even on paper, is a great way to learn from your experience and mistakes. When you put that journal online, you benefit from the insights of other knitters who post comments to your blog. You can even ask for particular tips or suggestions on your blog.

When I spoke to Debbie Stoller, she suggested that in a society where knitters are still in the minority—only one in three women knows how to knit—blogs establish knitting communities that were once easier to form organically.

"In the past, in communities of women, they all knew how to knit, and you could make something and show it to everyone," Stoller said. "We're getting so disconnected from this women's work and never having an opportunity to share."

Even with the knitting boom, Stoller said she suspects the average female friend might not appreciate the work that goes into making a sweater. "I think that, still, if you had knit a sweater for a friend they'd say, 'Uh, that's nice,' and if it's not quite their size they'd never wear it," Stoller said. "They may think that it took you a couple of days." (A sweater usually takes several weeks of regular knitting for even a fast knitter to complete.)

"The only person who's going to appreciate all the work that went into (a sweater) is someone who knits," Stoller said. "Now we have to actively get out and seek that person. It's all about finding a community. You want to share it with someone who gets it."

Kay Gardiner of Mason-Dixon Knitting shared that sentiment. Gardiner said about knitting, "I think it's such a solitary thing. Sometimes I'm wearing my new sweater, and nobody in my house notices I'm wearing my new sweater, and nobody noticed that I'd been working on it for five months. You want a meaningful acknowledgement of what you've done, and you get that (through blogging)."

I met some urban knitters who were decidedly against blogging, so I asked them why. Elinore Kaufman of Knitters for Choice said she found the confessional content of some blogs boring and depressing.[9]

"I like looking at people's knitting projects, but I don't like reading blogs," Kaufman said. "I guess I just don't really want to hear what people I don't know did that day. And I don't really like reading bad writing. And I'm worried there are some aspects of my personality that would make me the kind of person who would have a blog, but I don't really want to add to the madness."

Blogging holds particular charms for the rural knitter and for homemakers, and Stoller said she finds this correlation telling. "What I think is interesting is that a lot of people with the most active blogs are stay-at-home moms," Stoller said. "I think about how Betty Friedan wrote about that (malaise that some housewives feel) as the problem that has no name."

Homemakers, particularly those with young children, can end up isolated in a way that women working outside the home are not, Stoller noted. "In a way, blogging gets you an audience besides your husband and kids to say, 'You did a good job,'" she said.

Sabrina Gschwandtner, fiber artist and creator of the fiber arts magazine *KnitKnit*, said she has given a lot of thought to why knitters blog.[10] "For a lot of knitters, blogging serves a very essential function—they want to share (their knitting) with people, and they want to keep it going," Gschwandtner said. "It motivates people to keep going. They get comments and feedback. You tap into this Internet community. If you're a knitter who doesn't have much of a community . . . you can blog about it and people will encourage you."

Gschwandtner also discussed how certain blogs give knitters an opportunity to criticize knitting designers. On the blog You Knit What?, which stopped being published during the summer of 2006, bloggers posted photos of designs in order to mock them, either for their alleged impracticality, ugliness, or ridiculousness. Criticism of knitting patterns can also be found in many blogs, and Gschwandtner, a former designer for high fashion knitwear, takes it to heart. She described the criticism as an example of how blogging can give too much authority to casual or amateur knitters and writers.

"When criticism and praise for designers is being published, it's usually from hobbyists who have a dream or a fantasy of being published, and it's kind of a little bit dangerous category of people who know a little bit about designing but not enough," Gschwandtner said. "They clearly don't fully understand what goes into designing a garment."

And yet, Gschwandtner hailed knitting for serving so many purposes for all kinds of practitioners of the craft. Amateurs can dabble in knitting as a profession by designing garments and either selling them or their patterns online. People who don't want to leave their day jobs can supplement their incomes. Mothers at home with children can develop cottage industries via the Internet.

"Knitting is so popular that it has spawned alternate distribution models," Gschwandtner said. "It's such a flexible medium, with all the professionals and hobbyists involved."

Brenda Dayne, who airs the knitting podcast Cast On, confessed that she wasn't interested in blogging until she learned that bloggers were linking to her podcast, helping it to become a tremendous success, with thousands of subscribers.[11]

"I really thought they were just for losers," Dayne said of blogs. "It's only been really since the podcast—they've been passing me along—they drew me into this thing that was part of a trend."

Gilbert (of Clapotis fame) first made Dayne aware of the wealth of knitting blogs when the two worked together on an interview of raw art knitter Marie Rose Lortet in Paris. (Gilbert, who speaks fluent French, translated Lortet's comments for Dayne.) At some point, Gilbert mentioned to Dayne her blog, called Needles on Fire (http://www.kategilbert.com/blog/).

Soon Dayne was convinced that blogs aren't just the realm of the bored or unemployed. Knitting bloggers have major promoting power. They spread the word about Cast On and help encourage thousands of listeners to subscribe to the podcast.

In New Haven, Stitch 'N Bitch member Bryna Subherwal said blogging takes the place of phone calls and letters to friends and family.[12] People who don't keep in touch with her can check her blog to see what she's doing, she said. She also blogs for her own enrichment, she said.

"On a personal level, it's more to keep writing," Subherwal said. "At my old job, I thought the writing would be more substantive than it was. I thought I would at least be writing memorandums. It's to have something to write about that I care about writing about, and to encourage self-reflection. I've written in a journal less since I started blogging."

Fellow New Haven knitter Jessica Lang wrote in a post about why people blog on her own blog, Zarzuela Knits and Crochets (http://www.zarzuela.blogspot.com). People who read the blog posted comments with their insights.[13] Most respondents said they blogged for themselves, but Lang told them on her blog that she doubted self-examination was their only motivation.

"If you just did it for yourself, you could keep a journal," Lang said. She believes record-keeping is one appealing element of blogging, "but it's the human interaction that's the biggest thing." Lang said she also enjoys the technical aspect of blogging.

Another member of the New Haven knitting club is Lauren Lax, who persuaded many of the other knitters in her circle to start blogs.[14] She professes that her main reason for starting a blog was to get advice on techniques.

"I'm not into self-reflection," said the Yale School of Management graduate student. Even rereading her old blog entries sometimes makes her uncomfortable, she said. Her blog, almostfelted.com (http://almostfelted.knitblog.com/) was born of sheer practicality. She simply wanted some knitting advice.

"I was knitting Charlotte's Web (a complex lace scarf) in Koigu (a hand-painted merino yarn) and wanted to know if people crocheted the edge before or after blocking," Lax said. (Blocking is the process of pinning a knitted garment to a flat surface and steaming or wetting it to force it into the right shape.)

Lax has been blogging since about 2002, she said. "At first I didn't know anyone who knit at all," Lax said. She has come to see her blog as a way to develop as large a community of knitting friends as possible.

"It really is a subculture," Lax said of the knitting community. "People are freaked out by the depth of vocabulary. You can say things in shorthand (to other knitters)."

While bloggers on the whole use a vast vocabulary of acronyms in their communications, knitting bloggers add even more shorthand to the mix. Here are some of the most common knitting blog acronyms: A work in progress is commonly called a WIP. KIP, short for knitting in public, often gets used as a verb, with suffixes attached, as in the sentence, "A whole bunch of people were KIPing on the subway this morning." A finished object is an FO. An LYS is a local yarn shop. Many new knitters prefer LYSs to big-box stores or large craft stores. This is because large stores typically do not sell a wide variety of high-end and natural fiber yarns but instead focus on acrylics and synthetic blends manufactured by large yarn companies. A UFO is an unfinished object. UFOs differ from WIPS in that a WIP is a project one is actively pursuing, while a UFO runs the risk of never getting finished. Other, more obscure knitting acronyms exist and can be very amusing, such as SABLE: stash acquisition beyond life expectancy. (Knitters typically view achieving SABLE as a good thing, but something to hide from nonknitting friends and family.) That's because few people, other than fellow knitters, can understand knitting obsession. Lax's predicament is a prime example of how people enthralled by knitting often function.

Lax's knitting world is almost like an underground for her. Her family doesn't know the extent of her knitting habit, and, for that reason, she doesn't tell them about her blog. The blog features a gallery of Lax's FOs. Several of those projects were jobs she did designing or test-knitting patterns for yarn companies. Lax is an accomplished knitter, and she started knitting professionally when she learned yarn producers would send her free yarn with which to create designs and knit samples for them. The items she knits for the companies must be relinquished, of course, but that doesn't matter much to Lax. She is a process knitter. She enjoys the act of knitting at least as much as the finished product.

"I didn't tell my boyfriend at first, either (about the blog)," Lax said as she whizzed through stitches on a self-designed crewneck sweater. "It bothers me that he doesn't have an interest in understanding what I do. He's playing a computer game right now. At least my hobby is productive."

ONLINE MAGAZINES AND WEB SITES

A handful of free online knitting magazines offer patterns, features, reviews of products, and tips on technique. The most influential of these, *Knitty* (http://www.knitty.com), has entertained more than 18.5 million visitors since its launch in September 2002. The success of this publication, edited by Amy Singer of Toronto, Canada, is remarkable.

Knitty's winter 2005 issue had 1.5 million visitors in the first month it was live, according to the site's web statistics. More than 30,000 people visit the site every day.

Knitty's success seems to defy odds. At the time of this writing, a heat wave enveloped much of North America, during which temperatures reached 100 degrees Fahrenheit and higher for days on end. Knitters typically enjoy their craft more when there's a chill in the air, and, in fact, many bloggers during the week in question wrote about their inability to continue projects in the oppressive heat. Even so, *Knitty*'s site meter counted nearly 10,000 visitors to the online magazine in a single hour on August 2, 2006.

Young knitters anxiously await each quarterly issue of *Knitty*. The writing is consistently clear, upbeat, and often humorous. The scores of patterns available for free download from *Knitty*'s archives are a healthy blend of trendy and traditional. Submissions come from a mix of established professional designers and hobbyists. *Knitty* pays all of them for their designs. The site's layout and design are modern and beautiful. Singer has her finger on the pulse of the knitting movement, so much so that she has also been hired to write a regular column on knitting and the Internet for *Interweave Knits*. Singer also reported in a 2006 issue that she was able to leave her former full-time job and support herself by editing *Knitty*.

Perhaps the most significant effect of *Knitty*'s popularity is the trend among amateur knitters to attempt to design patterns. Despite its professional sheen, *Knitty*'s great innovation is that it relies most heavily on designs by people who may have never been paid to create a knitting pattern before. The magazine maintains a huge readership because the patterns within it are consistently innovative, reliable, and attractive, regardless of origin. Furthermore, *Knitty* is not the sole domain of young, trendy knitters. Older, more traditional, and highly experienced knitters tend to enjoy *Knitty*, too.

Another popular knitting publication is *Knitter's Review*, the online project of Clara Parkes. For six years, the weekly newsletter has featured reviews of yarns, knitting books, tools, and other products related to knitting. While Parkes is never as blunt as the typical movie review critic when she assesses a product, she is extremely thorough and thoughtful in her analysis. Once familiar with the critic's voice, readers of *Knitter's Review* can recognize her subtle emphasis on the flaws of a given product. Parkes' honesty and care have garnered her an audience of about 30,000 loyal readers. *Knitter's Review* also hosts numerous knitting forums, where participants can find fellow knitters in their area, publicize local charity efforts, or simply chat.

A general interest, free online knitting magazine is *MagKnits*, the brainchild of British knitter Kerrie Allman. Allman, who also writes the blog Kerrie's Place (www.kerriesplace.co.uk), explains on the blog that she learned to knit as a child but became an avid knitter in 2000, while pregnant with her first child. She had a few designs published in *Knitty* before she decided to launch her own online knitting magazine, which she says receives about 10,000 hits a day.

Male knitters have their own haven at Men Who Knit (www. MenWhoKnit.com). This site, with about 585 users in September 2006, attracts a large gay audience and features more chat than patterns. A second site for male knitters is Men Knit (www.menknit.net), which largely offers encouragement for men to take up the craft. The most developed page features a brief history of male knitting.

Among the newer and more popular online magazines that feature knitting is *The AntiCraft* (www.theanticraft.com), a Gothic-themed crafting site.

The AntiCraft is the invention of two young women in Kentucky, Zabet Stewart and Renée Rigdon. By day, Zabet (or Elizabeth, as her mother knows her) is a web designer for the University of Kentucky. Rigdon is a stay-at-home mom with a son.

They have a secret: they aren't really Goths. That is, they don't dye their hair black, wear all-black clothing, cover their faces with paste-white foundation makeup, and line their eyes and lips in black. They don't listen to an inordinate amount of dark, brooding alternative music, either.

"I think we're just bitter, honestly," said Stewart in an interview with this author. "We were kind of Goth in high school. Well, I went to a high school that didn't have a Gothic subculture, but if it did, I would have liked them. I didn't fit in. I was a total outcast. I mostly hung out with the AV (audiovisual) geeks."

Rigdon attended the same high school as Stewart, but four years later. "They had Goths by the time I was in high school," Rigdon said. "But I didn't really fit in with them. I was too lazy to wash my blacks every day and put on the makeup."

What they lack in Gothic appearance, they make up for in attitude. Stewart claims her bitterness should compensate for her dearth of black clothing. "I hate everybody," Stewart said with a laugh. "Mostly, people will say, 'I love mankind in general, but a couple of people are real assholes.' I say, 'I hate mankind in general.'"

"We don't fit in exactly with the punks, Goths, depressed people, angry people—all that," she said. "We're realists with a pessimist bent." The two friends got the idea to launch *The AntiCraft* during a knitting circle, they said.

"We were sitting around with a couple of other knitters talking about those 'Bad Girls' Guide to Knitting' books and thought, 'Wouldn't it be cool to have a Goth Girl's Guide to Knitting?'" Stewart said.

"We threw this idea around for a couple of minutes, maybe a half hour and I kept thinking about it. I started illustrating then got encouragement from our local Stitch 'N Bitch group (in Lexington, Kentucky). Debbie Stoller came through Cincinnati and we kind of stalked her and took her to dinner. She was really cool about it. We asked her about what was involved with writing a book, and came to the conclusion it was too hard."

The two women thought they could keep more control over the creative process by publishing a Web site, particularly with Stewart's web design skills. Rigdon started test knitting like crazy.

In their site's Antifesto, *The AntiCraft* women made clear their disdain for mainstream crafting. "No more would we be cowed into silence by cheerful scrapbook stickers. Never again would we be forced to gleefully execute a sweater of intarsia puppies," they wrote. "Really, we thrilled that crafting was de-grannified; we just got tired of it having to be so dang perky all the time."

Stewart and Rigdon gave their readers projects that were slightly more sinister than most. A scarf pattern sports an intarsia image that morphs from a snowflake into a skull. Hollow doll parts are filled with soil to seed an herb garden. A knitted voodoo doll offers revenge for scorned lovers.

The AntiCraft women, self-described "strange girls," discovered quickly that they were not alone. "It's gone really well," Stewart said. Their blog tracker indicates that about a thousand people visit the site regularly.

About 20,000 people sought out the first issue, from as far away as Japan, Saudi Arabia, Norway, Germany, the United Kingdom, and Russia. Stewart said she thinks the surge in knitting's popularity is just a cyclical happening. Rigdon credited the Internet with bringing out the natural competitiveness in knitters.

"I think I agree with the Yarn Harlot, who says, 'It's not art. It's not craft. It's sport.' Knitters get really competitive. When one tries something new, others say, 'Maybe I could do that, and then more people start seeing it.'"

Both women said they think crafters will turn to another hobby eventually. They deliberately included a variety of crafts on *The Anti-Craft* so that the site will succeed even after knitting's heyday passes.

"I'm sure crochet will be the next big thing," Rigdon said. "You can call it the new yoga or whatever, but it's just cycles," Stewart said. "Personally, I'm waiting for grunge to come back. I can't wait for grunge to come back. I'm so sick of showering."

Even if knitting falls back out of fashion, Stewart and Rigdon said they will probably always feature some knitting on their site. "I'm probably always going to be knitter," Stewart said.

PODCASTS

Some people are better talkers than writers. Fortunately for them, technology has generated another media outlet for amateurs. In 2005, many would-be radio show hosts used their computers to create their own audio shows, called podcasts, syndicating their programs with an RSS. (The acronym stands for several different terms, among them, "really simple syndication," "rich site summary," and "RDF site summary," all of which represent file formats that allow Web sites, web blogs, and podcasts to syndicate.)

Little technical savvy is required to set up a podcast, according to Brenda Dayne, host of the popular knitting podcast, Cast On. Visitors to Apple's iTunes Web site can easily search for podcasts on a wide range of subjects.

During 2006, many knitters added their podcasts to those available free on iTunes, but only a few of these programs are able to make interesting use of the medium. The podcast is not quite as accommodating to knitters' needs as is the blog. A knitted project can be shown off in a photograph more easily than it can be described aurally. That said, a talented storyteller like Dayne can use the podcast to entertain, inform, and connect with other knitters. Marie Irshad, host of the podcast, KnitCast, specializes in interviews with known figures in the knitting world. But many new knitting podcasts fail to consider the medium and the interests of their audiences. In fact, some sound as though the hosts don't realize they are recording.

A handful of great podcasts set a high standard for others. Irshad was a pioneer of the genre. Her program, KnitCast, features interviews with knitting designers, artists, bloggers, and various other knitting celebrities. Irshad is a radio editor by day, and the sleek sound of her program benefits from her background. Her interviews have the air of a professional news broadcast.

Dayne's podcast may not be the first, but it is outstanding. Cast On is an aural forum where Dayne airs music to knit by. She uses pod-safe music; these are songs that bands allow podcasters to use for free. Dayne has a good ear for talent. She has a mellifluous voice that beckons you to listen to her regular "Sweater of the Day," program, describing the drama that ensued as she knit a particular sweater. She also airs an essay in each broadcast, where she loses some of her freestyle whimsy and waxes philosophical. It's hard to believe that Dayne's broadcasting education amounts to a single fifteen-minute lesson she received twenty-five years ago, during a brief stint in the U.S. Army.

Why create a podcast about the joys of knitting? Dayne said she started knitting a bit more than a decade ago, long before a trend was afoot.[15]

"Anything that smacked of trendiness, I would shy away from it," Dayne said.

When she noticed her hobby was catching on, she figured the knitting frenzy would be brief, she said.

"It was a bunch of novelty scarves," Dayne said. "I knew it was going to come and go. Until about three or four years ago I was insisting that the trend had peaked and it would go no further."

When the trend proved to be resilient, Dayne set about collecting her thoughts on the craft. "Part of why I started the podcast is all the thoughts I have about knitting," Dayne said. "Had I thought about the option of writing a book, I would have. I didn't think anybody would be interested in the philosophy of knitting."

"There are so many reasons why people do it," Dayne said. Dayne learned when a friend named Jean brought her knitting with her to a coffee date. Dayne asked the friend to knit her a sweater, not thoroughly understanding the work involved.

"She said, 'No, I won't make you a sweater, but I'll teach you how to knit,'" Dayne recalled. "She helped me to pick out the pattern and yarn." Dayne said that from her first attempt at making a knit stitch, she realized the process was magic.

"I was trained as a painter. I'd done calligraphy. But here were these unfamiliar tools. I was completely inept. Here was complete beginner's mind," she said. "From that first sweater I was absolutely hooked. I remember taking it with me everywhere."

Jean and Dayne's friendship was forged by knitting, though they were friends before. "We used to meet at each other's houses. We had our knitting group of just two. When she joined a Stitch 'N Bitch group that was founded in Portland she told me, 'I'm cheating on you!'"

Dayne laughed remembering how she would show off her very first rows of knitting and tell people it was a sweater. "It reminds me very much of what people do on blogs," she said.

She spent months collecting material for her podcast before she went on air on Halloween of 2005, compelled by a desire to use a song with a Halloween theme. "I was afraid to turn the mic on," Dayne said. "You really are alone in your house. You don't connect to the fact that there are 3,000 listeners a week that download the show. That's huge."

At the time Dayne was interviewed for this book, in February 2006, she was one of the most popular of all podcasts and blogs managed by FeedBurner. Fewer than 100 of FeedBurner's users have more than 1,000 subscribers, Dayne said.

Like others interviewed for this book, Dayne attributed the technological savvy of many young knitters to their yen to communicate about their beloved hobby. Dayne's own life has been changed dramatically by technology. A divorced mother of a college-aged son, Dayne met her partner, a Welsh woman, online eight years ago. The women were friends who wrote to each other every day. When her e-mail friend visited her in Portland, Oregon, Dayne realized she was in love. Dayne moved to Wales to live with her partner in 2000. Since then, the Internet has allowed her to stay in touch with friends in the United States.

She says that if you don't have that sort of community or yarn shops locally, the Internet can be an important way to connect with other knitters. "I have the one LYS," she said. That shop carries only two brands that she favors, but it's better than nothing.

Dayne has been on a knitting mailing list for about eight or nine years. She isn't very close to people on the list, but she finds it comforting to see the same names on the list year after year. They are great knitters to consult for information on techniques.

Dayne said she believes the rapid evolution of media will soon allow broadcasters like her to force a paradigm switch in which they will be able to be highly selective in choosing advertisers for their venue.

"In five years you'll be walking around with your cell phone and you'll be able to stream video through, essentially, a broadband," Dayne said. "The world of media will change, as we know it. I think there's an opportunity here to switch the paradigm. I want to look for sponsorship by somebody whose products I represent. That's where the politics come in. I want to walk the talk. . . . I'll be a verbal sponsorship. There will be no Monsanto, no Wal-Mart, no Enron."

Instead, Dayne said, she'll promote only products that she truly loves, like a small Welsh whisky shop that she claims makes the best single malt scotch, or Lakeland Limited, a company that makes kitchen and craft supplies.

In just the first half of 2006, more than a dozen new podcasts became available on the iTunes Music Store, and others started up that were accessible through related blogs. Few of these shows are as professional or interesting as Dayne's or Irshad's. And yet, the proliferation of broadcasts in this new genre demonstrates that knitting continues to excite young people around the globe.

One enjoyable listen is Insubordiknit, the podcast of a heavily tattooed knitting mother in Baltimore, Maryland, named Jacey Boggs. Boggs, who was thirty-one when she first aired her podcast in May 2006, is gifted at spinning a yarn, both literally and figuratively. She wisely established regular sections to her biweekly show, including "Who's That Purl?" which profiles a knitter and "This Knitter's Life," which tells a story about a knitter, but not only about knitting. Boggs said in her maiden broadcast that she intended to focus on knitters rather than knitting. She likes to talk about how knitting is meaningful to her, and she draws analogies between her craft and life in general. It helps, too, that Boggs speaks conscientiously and uses pleasing or surprising sounds to add interest; a background of crickets or chirping frogs might accompany her soothing voice. Her son is occasionally called upon to read brief segments in the podcast's script.

ONLINE STORES

Though nothing can match the heady bliss of an actual yarn store visit, a bevy of online yarn sellers ensures that smart shoppers can usually find even rare and discontinued yarns, and at the best price. Many actual yarn stores have virtual shops online, while other shops are purely Internet-based. EBay, the online auction house, is a venue for home spinners and dyers to ply their wares. The online auction house also lets knitters unload overabundant stashes.

Local yarn shops, particularly the independent ones favored by many young knitters, often have to limit the brands of yarn they sell because companies may require that they buy a minimum quantity of their product. Yarn companies sometimes also limit the number of retail sellers in a geographical area to whom they will sell, in order to avoid oversaturating the market. These economic facts can make it hard for a knitter to locate the particular yarn she wants. Or, at least, that was the case until the recent proliferation of online yarn outlets.

What was once a knitter's nightmare—running out of yarn before completing a project—is today a problem that can usually be resolved quickly. A knitter can find extra skeins of most yarns, even discontinued ones, either by inquiring with shops around the globe or by asking fellow knitters through web blogs and e-mail list servers.

9

JUST ONE MORE ROW! WHAT'S NEXT FOR KNITTERS AND KNITTING

The nature of a trend is that it eventually dies out. This is as true for the knitting revival that began in the mid-1990s as it is for any trend. In time, the attention of the media and knitting dilettantes will move elsewhere. The buzz in crafting circles is that crochet is the new knitting. That rumor may have something to do with the 2006 publication of Debbie Stoller's most recent book, *Stitch 'N Bitch Crochet: The Happy Hooker.*

Alas for my own book sales, I suspect the knitting trend is already on its way out. While a communications specialist for one of the world's leading management consulting firms McKinsey & Company, I learned a little something about trends. It seems that when a trend hits its peak among mainstream Americans—kids in the suburbs and in rural Midwestern towns—that trend is on the decline. This is a fairly obvious phenomenon. After all, when everybody's doing something, it isn't really cool anymore, is it? The trendy activity, be it roller skating, skate boarding, getting a tattoo or a piercing, listening to "alternative" music, becomes just something that people do. The once trendy activity may remain something that helps the average teenager develop a sense of belonging and identity. But that activity can't remain hip forever.

An August 2006 article in *Publisher's Weekly*[1] asked whether knitting was heading toward becoming a widespread activity or if the trend would soon fizzle out. Evidence led to mixed conclusions: while yarn shops still exist in trendy neighborhoods and hip, edgy knitting books often outnumber traditional ones in modern bookstores, sales of knitting books remain popular, but have slowed since 2003.

Lackluster yarn sales may also indicate that the knitting trend is waning. Mary Colucci, executive director of the Craft Yarn Council of America, said yarn retailers seem to be disappointed with this year's profits. "I don't know if sales are what people expected them to be, because people have so many more choices," Colucci said.[2]

Even so, knitting provides such advantages to young, busy people today that I believe many will continue to ply their yarn and needles after the hubbub dies down. The pleasure one gets from knitting is enduring. People don't necessarily knit because everyone else is doing it. As a pastime, knitting is more like smoking than, say, inline skating. Beyond being fun, knitting is also easy, portable, and addictive. And yet, unlike smoking, knitting is truly relaxing and not carcinogenic.

Kay Gardiner of the blog Mason-Dixon Knitting speculated that knitting might blossom into a pervasive mainstream activity, much as gourmet cooking did after chef Julia Child popularized the activity with her books and television show.

"Before Julia Child, people usually only had two cookbooks—Fanny Farmer and The Joy of Cooking," Gardiner said. "Now everybody's got fifty cookbooks, not because they're cooking, but because it's enjoyable. It has gone from something necessary to something you feel pleasure about."

Or, knitting may not have such universal appeal. Not everyone will understand the attraction of the craft, and many may not be able to master it. Knitters often repeat the platitude, "It's not rocket science," but neither is knitting, particularly advanced knitting, a skill that everyone has the patience or ability to learn.

Gardiner suspects, though, that many of the knitters who picked up the habit during its most recent heyday will keep it up, learning ever more complex and interesting techniques.

"I think those hard core knitters that are doing it and have been doing it since the craze started got addicted, and they are going to keep knitting," Gardiner said. "Knitting lives up to the hype. It is an endlessly interesting thing that you can do your whole life."

Here is some evidence that knitting has hit the mainstream (and, if marketing history can be trusted, is losing its trendiness).

New York City's Museum of Arts and Design (MAD) slated for January 2007 to September 2008 a traveling exhibition called *Radical Lace and Subversive Knitting*, which would include the works of twenty-seven international artists who use knitting and other fiber arts as their medium.

Knitting clubs are all the rage in the suburbs and in rural areas as I complete this book. In Bethlehem, Pennsylvania, known nationally as a depressed steel town, young knitters gather monthly in a local yarn store called Tangled Yarns.

In Pennsylvania's largely rural Lehigh Valley, a knitting group formed in July 2006, advertising itself through the online service, Meetup.com. The group's organizer noted, "The largest spot on the farm for gatherings is on the threshing floor in the barn."

With independent yarn shops springing up even in small, middle-class to working-class towns, the fiber market may be close to glutted. No doubt, the free market system will prevail, and some fiber and knitting-related businesses will not last long. At the same time, smart entrepreneurs who have prepared for change are likely to thrive.

Shop owners like Lauren Gorman of Three Black Sheep in Northport, New York planned for the eventual end of the knitting fad. Gorman said she and her partners never set out to be a scarf shop, that is, a place that sells mostly novelty yarns. She and other yarn store owners heeded CYCA's advice to cultivate the new generation of avid knitters by offering a wide array of classes at various times of day and experience levels. Gorman believes that many people who jumped on the scarf-knitting bandwagon are eager to develop more skills. "You have to offer them something," she said.

The sheer volume and variety of knitting books on the market today attests to the popularity of the craft. The Yarn Harlot isn't the only writer to use knitting metaphors as the basis for writing in a genre other than "how-to."

Novelist Debbie MacComber has made *The New York Times* bestseller list with her story about people in a knitting circle, *A Good Yarn*. Maggie Sefton's mysteries with a knitting theme include the novels, *Knit One, Kill Two*, *A Deadly Yarn*, and *Died in the Wool*, as well as an earlier collection of stories entitled *Needled to Death*.

A slew of new knitting books target the youth market. There's *Teen Knitting Club: Chill Out and Knit* by Jennifer Wenger, *Kids Knitting* by Melanie Falick, *Kids Knit: Simple Steps to Happy Projects* by Sarah Bradberry, and *Kids Can Knit* by Carolyn Clewer.

Aimee Strause, a woman in her young twenties living in Sellersville, Pennsylvania, said she learned to knit in 2004 while a counselor at nearby Bear Creek Camp. Another counselor taught her and lots of other people at the camp. Strause has been knitting steadily since then. She has accumulated a small library of knitting books through a book club, as well as a healthy stash of novelty yarns she bought from major craft stores. Strause, a student of conservation at Delaware Valley College, said when she has time to spare from studying, she wants to develop her knitting skills, learning more advanced stitches and finally tackling a sweater.

In Quakertown, Pennsylvania, where I live, a charity called Stitches of Love that knits garments for needy mothers of new babies, including wraps for stillborn children, has expanded to teach children to knit.

Barbara Grove co-founded the organization with Beth Supplee in 2003 at Providence Presbyterian Church in Quakertown. Grove explained the origins of the group while she knitted up a cream-colored baby sweater, sitting with perfect posture at a project table in a church basement, wearing an impeccable navy suit and pearls. She was at a benefit event for Quakertown's Crossroads Pregnancy Care, a Christian-based center where abortion is discouraged and post-abortion counseling is provided. Grove said it struck her that people ought to be doing more to support young women after they have been encouraged to keep their babies. "That's when they need the most support," Grove said. "And there's a lot of poverty around these communities."

Three years later, Stitches of Love has expanded to include more than 800 members aged 5 to 102, who knit in churches, senior centers, schools, and at home. They make clothing, blankets, quilts, and dolls using all kinds of needlework techniques, and recipients of their gifts are widespread. At a meeting I attended at Peace Lutheran Church in Perkasie, Pennsylvania, one member thrilled at a photo she received of a little girl on a Native American reservation near Scottsdale, Arizona, grinning and hugging a doll the member had made.

Knitting lessons for children were slated to begin in October 2006 at Providence Presbyterian Church and at the Quakertown YMCA. "The earlier you teach the children you're here to serve, the better they'll be," Grove said.

Originally, many Stitches of Love members were women in middle age or older. This club's expansion to include younger women and girls reflects, in my view, a heartening progression of the knitting movement.

The organization was formed because a group of older women felt compelled to reach out to young women in need. Now, younger people are sharing the responsibility, but they are also sharing the fun of the craft and the companionship it provides. Stitches of Love meetings allow a diverse group of people to become friends and share their love of craft, including men and children. At least in this instance, the development of the knitting community into one that includes every age group and gender has come full circle.

The fun of knitting has been the secret behind the craft's endurance all along: though it is surely a functional activity, it is also a relaxing, enjoyable, and even magical one. You cannot truly understand this secret until you try knitting for yourself, but once you do, you are likely to be hooked.

Gardiner imagines that, given the chance, her former colleagues at the U.S. Attorney's office in Manhattan would express puzzlement over the life she has centered on knitting.

"They would say, 'What are you doing?'" Gardiner said. "They can't understand it. You will only get it if you ever do it yourself and it has the same effect on you."

If this book does not persuade you, in the words of Yarn Harlot, Stephanie Pearl-McPhee, "of how much fun we're all having," then I hope you will give knitting a try for yourself. In a perfect world, everyone would be a member of this close-knit circle.

NOTES

CHAPTER 1

1. Barbara G. Walker, *A Treasury of Knitting Patterns* (Pittsville, WI: Schoolhouse Press, 1998), 3–4.

2. Richard Rutt, *A History of Hand Knitting* (London: B.T. Batsford, 1987), 32.

3. Irena Turnau, *History of Knitting Before Mass Production*, trans. Agnieszka Szonert (Warsaw: Institute of the History of Material Culture, Polish Academy of Sciences, 1991), 10.

4. Rutt, 58.

5. Turnau, 16–18.

6. Ibid., 62.

7. Ibid., 25.

8. Ibid., 29.

9. Dominican Sisters of the Presentation, *Blessed Marie Poussepin Historical Facts*, http://www.dominicansistersofthepresentation.org/blessed_marie_poussepin.htm (accessed September 13, 2006).

10. Turnau, 73.

11. Rutt, 62.

12. Joan Thirsk, "The Fantastical Folly of Fashion: The English Stocking Knitting Industry 1500–1700," in *Textile History and Economic History: Essays in Honour of Julia de Lacey Mann*, ed. N.B. Harte and K.G. Ponting (Manchester, UK: Manchester University Press, 1973), 50–73, as cited by Rutt, 77.

13. Owen Osborne, *The Story of the Stocking* (Philadelphia: Owen Osborne, 1927), 14, as cited in Anne L. Macdonald, *No Idle Hands: The Social History of American Knitting* (New York: Ballantine Books, 1988), 5.

14. Turnau, 40.

15. Ibid., 42.

16. Rutt, 223.

17. Kazekobo (knitwear designer Yoko Hatta), *History of Knitting in Japan, Part 1*, knitjapan, www.knitjapan.co.uk (accessed September 6, 2006). The designer cites as her main source, Yoshihiro Matushita, *Amimono ima mukashi (Knitting Today & Past)* (Tokyo: Nihon Vogue: 1986).

18. The text of President Fillmore's letter to the Emperor of Japan, U.S. Senate. 33rd Cong., 2nd sess., Exec. Docs. #34 (1854–5), Vol. 6, 9–11, as cited by Joseph V. O'Brien, Department of History, John Jay College of Criminal Justice, http://web.jjay.cuny.edu/jobrien/reference/ob54.html (accessed September 6, 2006).

19. *(Williamsburg) Virginia Gazette*, September 12, 1771, as cited by Macdonald, 5.

20. Adam Smith, *An Inquiry into the Nature and Causes of the Wealth of Nations*, 5th ed., cited from Edwin Cannan's annotated edition (London: Methuen, 1904), 53.

21. Macdonald, 6.

22. Mellon Chamberlain, *The American Revolution: A Narrative, Critical, and Bibliographical History* (n.p.: Land's End Press, 1972).

23. Macdonald, 29.

24. Ibid., 34.

25. Edith Patterson Meyer, *Petticoat Patriots of the American Revolution* (New York: Vanguard Press, 1976), 86–87, as cited in Macdonald, 37.

26. Maria Mitchell, *Growing up Female in America: Ten Lives*, ed. Eve Merriam (New York: Dell, 1973), 77.

27. Macdonald, 104–105.

28. Mark Overton, *Agricultural Revolution in England 1500–1850*, BBC, http://www.bbc.co.uk/history/british/empire_seapower/agricultural_revolution_02.shtm (accessed September 19, 2002).

29. Macdonald, 209–211.

30. Ibid., 252–253.

31. Ibid., 265.

32. Abra Edelman, *Celebrity Scarves* (New York: Sixth & Spring Books, 2003).

33. Macdonald, 284–286.

34. Ibid., 294.

35. Ibid., 298.

36. Ibid., 302.

37. Betty Friedan, *The Feminine Mystique* (New York: W.W. Norton, 1963).

38. Meg Swansen, *Meg Swansen's Knitting* (Loveland, CO: Interweave Press, 1999).

39. Elizabeth Zimmermann, *Knitting Workshop* (Pittsville, WI: Schoolhouse Press, 1981).

40. Art Hackett, producer, *Knitting Camp*, Wisconsin Public Television, December 22, 2005.

41. Rutt, 205, and Mary Walker Phillips: Fine Art in Stitches, Fresno Art Museum, www.fresnoartmuseum.org (accessed September 6, 2006).

CHAPTER 2

1. Mary Colucci, interview by author, August 22, 2006.
2. Debbie Stoller, *Stitch 'N Bitch: The Knitter's Handbook* (New York: Workman, 2003).
3. Debbie Stoller, interview by author, February 28, 2006.

CHAPTER 3

1. Ross Wetzsteon, *Republic of Dreams Greenwich Village: The American Bohemia, 1910–1960* (New York: Simon and Schuster, 2002).
2. National Public Radio's Talk of the Nation: Pop Culture. *Inside the World of Do-It-Yourself*, host Andrea Seabrook, December 28, 2005. Seabrook spoke with Mark Frauenfelder, editor of *Make* magazine and Shoshana Berger, editor of *ReadyMade* magazine.
3. Bryna Subherwal, interview by author, April 27, 2006.
4. Lauren Gorman, interview by author, April 25, 2006.
5. Jesse Loesberg, interview by author, May 5, 2006.
6. Jean Railla, *My Crafty Manifesto*, Web site and blog, getcrafty.com.
7. Cat Mazza, www.microRevolt.org, *About Us*.
8. Ibid., interview by author, September 18, 2006.
9. David Von Drehle, *Triangle: The Fire That Changed America* (New York: Atlantic Monthly Press, 2003).
10. Katie Franceschi, interview by author, May 18, 2006.
11. Lynn Wilson, interview by author, May 5, 2006.
12. Lauren Gorman, interview by author, April 25, 2006.

CHAPTER 4

1. Friedan, 15–32.
2. Jean Railla, *Feminism and the New Domesticity: My Crafty Manifesto*, getcrafty.com (accessed November 2, 2004).
3. Stoller, 7.
4. Stephanie Pearl-McPhee, interview by author, August 22, 2006.
5. Zoe Williams, "Close Knit," Guardian Weekend Magazine, January 8, 2005.
6. Sachin Shivaram, interview by author, May 1, 2006.
7. Kathy Lindbeck, interview by author, May 1, 2006.
8. Zabet Stewart, interview by author, July 6, 2006.

CHAPTER 5

1. Joanne Muzzin, interview by author, April 27, 2006.
2. Jessica Lang, interview by author, April 27, 2006.

3. Lauren Lax, interview by author, April 27, 2006.

4. Elinore Kaufman, interview by author, February 26, 2006.

5. Selma Miriam, interview by author, February 1, 2006.

6. Stephanie Pearl-McPhee, interview by author, August 30, 2006.

7. Maria Alvarez, interview by author, February 26, 2006.

8. Suyen Lyn, interview by author, January 20, 2006.

9. Freddie Robins, interview by Marie Irshad, KnitCast 18, December 7, 2005.

10. Beth Rosenberg, Eyebeam Journal: Dissecting Art and Technology, *In Conversation with Cat Mazza, Part I of II*, March 15, 2005.

11. Jesse Loesberg, *The Subversive Qualities of Male Knitting*, KQED-FM, July 5, 2003.

12. Jesse Loesberg, interview by author, May 5, 2006.

13. Bill Davenport, "Better than a Sweater: Montrose Taggers Are a Tight-knit Crew/Graffiti Is a Public Display of Affection for These Women," *Houston Chronicle*, February 21, 2006.

14. Sabrina Gschwandtner, interview by author, May 18, 2006.

15. Lucia Herndon, "Knitting to Dispel the Fear: You Can Calm Your Nerves While You Knit for Charities," *Philadelphia Inquirer Features Magazine*, October 3, 2001, pg. E03.

16. Suss Cousins, *Hollywood Knits Style: With 30 Original Suss Cousins Designs* (New York: Stewart, Tabori & Chang, 2004).

17. Loesberg, interview by author, May 5, 2006.

18. Pearl-McPhee, interview by author, August 22, 2006.

19. Sue Green, "The Knitting Revolution," *Craft Victoria*, www.craftculture.org.

20. Michele Hatty, "In the Loop: Knitters Yearn for Yarn and Companionship in a World of Uncertainty," *USA Today*, April 7, 2002.

21. BBC News, "Celebrity Knitting 'Sparks Boom,'" December 5, 2005 (accessed September 6, 2006).

CHAPTER 6

1. Gschwandtner, interview by author, May 18, 2006.

2. Gschwandtner, "Bags from Bags: Excerpts from an Interview with Jamie Petersen," *KnitKnit*, Issue 1, December 2002.

3. Marie Irshad, *KnitCast 18: Freddie Robins*, KnitCast podcast, December 7, 2005.

4. Freddie Robins, interview by author, May 1, 2006.

5. Victoria and Albert Museum Web site, Knit a Work of Art from a Free Pattern: "Conrad" Gloves by Freddie Robins, http://www.vam.ac.uk/collections/fashion/knitting/download/index.html.

6. Polly Leonard, "Freddie Robins' Subversive Sweaters," *Embroidery* 54, no. 2, 2003.

7. Cast Off Knitting Club for Boys and Girls, http://www.castoff.info/.

8. John D. Spiak, Arizona State University Art Museum gallery guide, *Mark Newport, Super Heroics*, June 25–September 3, 2005.

9. Lisa Anne Auerbach, http://www.stealthissweater.com/.

CHAPTER 7

1. "Knitting Goes Down Badly at The Savoy," *Evening Standard*, April 28, 2003.

2. Charlotte Higgins, "Political Protest Turns to the Radical Art of Knitting," *The Guardian*, January 31, 2005.

3. Marie Irshad, KnitCast 18: Freddie Robins, December 7, 2005.

4. Sabrina Gschwandtner, interview by author, May 18, 2006.

5. Jennifer Wang, interview by author, April 27, 2006.

6. Bryna Subherwal, interview by author, April 27, 2006.

7. Lauren Lax, interview by author, April 27, 2006.

8. Jennifer Koenig, interview by author, February 1, 2006.

9. Jesse Loesberg, interview by author, May 5, 2006.

10. Amy Singer, "Hi. A Letter of Introduction from the Editor, Amy R. Singer," *Knitty*, fall 2002.

11. Maria Alvarez and Elinore Kaufman, interview by author, November 13, 2005.

12. Laura Sponseller, interview by author, May 1, 2006.

13. Lucia Herndon, "New Strands of Kindness," *Philadelphia Inquirer Features Magazine*, March 30, 2005, city edition D, sec. C, 3.

14. Ibid., "Knitting to Dispel the Fear," *Philadelphia Inquirer Features Magazine*, October 3, 2001, city edition D, sec. E, 3.

15. Catherine Hollingsworth, "Put Needles to Work Spreading a Little Peace this Season," *Anchorage Daily News*, December 27, 2005.

16. The Dulaan Project Web site, http://www.fireprojects.org/dulaan.htm.

CHAPTER 8

1. Dave Sifry, "State of the Blogosphere, February 2006, Part 2, Beyond Search," posted on *Technorati*, February 14, 2006.

2. Stephanie Pearl-McPhee, interview by author, August 30, 2006.

3. Kay Gardiner and Ann Shayne, *Mason-Dixon Knitting: The Curious Knitter's Guide* (New York: Potter Craft, 2006).

4. Wendy D. Johnson, *Wendy Knits! My Never-ending Adventures in Yarn* (n.p., Plume: 2006).

5. Wendys Who Knit, home of Knitting Wendys netring, http://knittingwendys.blogspot.com/.

6. Kate Gilbert, interview by author, August 14, 2006.

7. Stephanie Pearl-McPhee, "Not Falling for It," *Yarn Harlot*, February 2, 2005.

8. Now Norma Knits, http://nownormaknits2.typepad.com/now_norma_knits_2/charity_knitting/index.html, posted August 1, 2006.

9. Elinore Kaufman, interview by author, February 26, 2006.

10. Sabrina Gschwandtner, interview by author, May 18, 2006.

11. Brenda Dayne, interview by author, February 14, 2006.

12. Bryna Subherwal, interview by author, April 27, 2006.

13. Jessica Lang, interview by author, April 27, 2006.

14. Lauren Lax, interview by author, April 27, 2006.

15. Brenda Dayne, interview by author, February 14, 2006.

CHAPTER 9

1. Natalie Danford, "The End of the Yarn?," *Publisher's Weekly*, August 28, 2006.

2. Mary Colucci, interview by author, August 22, 2006.

SELECTED RESOURCES

This is by no means a comprehensive guide to the book world and Internet's bounty of knitting resources, nor could it be. The number and variety of Web sites devoted to knitting is vast and grows daily, and great new books on knitting keep coming out.

Some of the very best, classic books on knitting technique are not featured on this list. If those are what you seek, look for titles by legends like Barbara Walker, Elizabeth Zimmerman, Meg Swansen, Kaffe Fassett, and Alice Starmore, for starters. The titles listed here are eye candy and provide an introduction to the craft—books published in recent years that helped inspire the current knitting revival.

Included here are Web sites I hope you will find interesting, funny, enlightening, unusual, or useful as you further explore the quirky, and yet, tradition-steeped world of America's young knitters. I have noted a few sites that sell patterns, knitwear, or yarns. None of these sellers have paid me, and I can't guarantee you will agree with my taste, which tends toward funky. With that stated, I wish you happy surfing.

BOOKS

Bliss, Debbie, *Special Knits: 22 Gorgeous Handknits for Babies and Toddlers* (North Pomfret, VT: Trafalgar Square Publishing, 2005).

Knitting a baby sweater is particularly satisfying for a new knitter, because one gets to learn sweater-making techniques without investing a ton in time and yarn to finish the project. Young knitters today, even those without kids, often find themselves making tiny garments for the children of friends and family. Bliss' instructions are easy to follow, and her close-up shots of rosy cheeks and tiny toes swathed in pastel hand-knits are enough to give even a man a passing yen to get pregnant.

Falick, Melanie, *Weekend Knitting: 50 Unique Projects and Ideas* (New York: STC Craft, 2003).

Weekend Knitting can fairly be called porn for knitters. Gratuitous pleasures of *Weekend Knitting* include recipes for hot chocolate, sugar cookies, and the perfect bath—all suggested as compliments to knitting during an ideal weekend. Beautiful, wholesome models are photographed in dreamy settings, appearing as perfect as the reader would like to look in the book's hand-knit designs. One may idly leaf through this book more often than one uses patterns within it, but one is unlikely to regret buying it.

Hoverson, Joelle, *Last-Minute Knitted Gifts* (New York: STC Craft, 2004).

Hoverson attended Yale College of Art before opening Purl yarn shop in New York City's chic SoHo neighborhood. Her art background, including a sophisticated approach to color, is evident in this beautifully photographed collection of projects. Hoverson alleges most projects can be completed in eight hours or fewer. Not every project is a good candidate for last-minute knitting; I knitted constantly through the 2005 Newport Folk Festival and still didn't complete the gorgeous chevron scarf. (And yet, I loved the scarf so much that, when I did finish it, I immediately began knitting another.) This book also offers a good explanation of color theory and how to apply it to one's knitting.

Macdonald, Anne L., *No Idle Hands: The Social History of American Knitting* (New York: Ballantine Books, 1988).

This book was one of my primary resources for the first chapter. It is also an atypically refreshing read. Macdonald introduces the idea that women have used knitting as a medium through which to express themselves even in times when social norms kept them from participating as actively as men in realms of political and social power. Podcaster Brenda Dayne mentioned to me that she learned how to knit without looking at her handiwork so that she could read this book at the same time. Pick it up, and you will understand why.

Stoller, Debbie, *Stitch 'N Bitch: The Knitter's Handbook* (New York: Workman, 2003).

This is, arguably, the book that started the modern knitting revival in earnest. Stoller's introduction explains her ideas about how knitting and other domestic activities should be embraced by feminists. Her instructions on knitting techniques are clear and easy to follow, and the patterns she collected from Stitch 'N Bitchers throughout the nation typify the new knitter's aesthetic.

WEB SITES

Alchemy Yarns of Transformation, http://www.alchemyyarns.com/.

I could eat this yarn. The colors are incredibly intense. The fibers are irresistibly touchable. Many larger companies create beautiful yarns, but Alchemy, produced at a farm in Northern California, draws my interest because it seems to be drenched with good intentions. Among their earth-friendly products is a yarn made of bamboo, a vegan fiber source that grows prolifically. Yes, the hues are trippy. You may not find that perfect neutral shade for knitting a tank shell to wear under a conservative suit jacket. You will please young children and your own inner child, though, if you make something playful with this yarn. Alchemy also sells many patterns that work well with its fibers, reflecting the same wild sense of imagination.

Almost Felted, http://almostfelted.knitblog.com/.

Almost Felted is the blog of a talented knitter I met at the New Haven, Connecticut Stitch 'N Bitch, Lauren Lax. She explicitly asked me not to identify her along with her blog name, for fear her family would harass her about her constant knitting, and yet, I couldn't resist. (Sorry, Lauren.) Lax is a student at Yale School of Management who ingeniously found a way to make her favorite hobby free: she designs and knits test patterns for yarn companies, which supply her yarn. Note her abundant gallery of finished objects (FOs). My favorite is a lovely tank designed for Alchemy called, "Ingenue."

Annie Modesitt, http://www.anniemodesitt.com/.

Annie Modesitt is a remarkably inventive knitting designer whose claim to fame is that she doesn't knit like most people do. She combines the motions of Western knitters (both English and Continental style) with those of Eastern knitting, practiced in Asia, Africa, South America, and Islamic countries, where knitting is believed to have originated. Modesitt's method is not unique; Mary Walker Phillips coined the phrase Combination Knitting to describe this style in her book, *Creative Knitting*. What's quite evident is that Modesitt's unconventional thinking allows her to create beautiful designs that are at once inventive and inspired by knitting tradition. Check out her gorgeous pattern for a Victorian corset tank top, which she vows will look good on a woman of any size. One can also link here to the designer's blog http://www.modeknit.com/blog/, which is not to be confused with an unrelated online retail establishment with a similar name, modeknits.com.

The AntiCraft, http://www.theanticraft.com/.

I love niches within niches. This is a Gothic online crafting magazine. Visit it when you want to knit a scarf whose pattern morphs from a snowflake into a skull, or to make your own coffin-shaped purse. For more on *The AntiCraft*, see Chapter 8.

Cast Off: Knitting Club for Boys and Girls, http://www.castoff.info/.

OK, so this isn't an American site, but the Internet makes our world much smaller. Don't deprive yourself of a visit to this Web site for London, England's knitting circle devoted to doing it in public. Cast Off organizes knitting parties at parks, clubs, bars, and even on the Underground. Members also revel in clever designs for items such as a knitted cigarette—an ad for it announces, "Look cool, stay healthy!" Knitted erotica include pasties, garters, and even a flesh-colored knitted penis, with cables posing as veins. Short movies on the site testify to the fun the group generates, and articles gathered there demonstrate how radical knitters can be.

Fuzzy Galore, http://www.fuzzygalore.biz/.

I was drawn to this site by "vegan fox," an irresistibly silly pattern for a faux fox stole, which *Knitty* published. The pattern, knitted entirely out of synthetic fiber, was modeled after the vintage sort of stole that used a real fox's little jaw, still in its head, as a clasp that grabbed its tail.

This is the site for all things fuzzy. Crystal Palace yarns, which the site's designers use exclusively, tend to have lots of furry, eyelashy, or otherwise interesting textures. The site is dedicated to the memory of Straw Into Gold, a San Francisco yarn store, now defunct, where the site developers learned to knit and were avid customers. Now the store owners have a wholesale business selling Crystal Palace yarns. Some of the felted projects are especially cute.

Fuzzy Galore takes its name from the character Pussy Galore in the James Bond flick, Goldfinger. One of the site's creators also has a very fluffy cat named Fuzzy Galore.

Get Crafty, http://getcrafty.com/index.php.

Get Crafty is the funky crafting Web site of Jean Railla, a New York City crafter and feminist. Her Crafty Manifesto offers a great introduction to the ethos of young, progressive DIY and domesticity enthusiasts. For more on getcrafty.com, see Chapter 3.

The Girl from Auntie, http://www.girlfromauntie.com/.

The sleek website of Jenna Wilson, a Toronto knitter with a fondness for The Avengers. The site takes its name from an episode of the sixties' television show in which agent Emma Peel is kidnapped and her cohort, John Steed, follows a trail of knitting needle-impaled corpses to discover the kidnapper, Grigorio Auntie, within the same building as a knitting circle. The title *The Girl from Auntie* is a play on *The Man from U.N.C.L.E.* Wilson supplies patterns for free and to buy, as well as a bunch of neat tools and techniques for knitters and a copyright guide for knitters. (Wilson has a day job as an intellectual property lawyer.)

Glampyre Knits, http://www.glampyre.com/blog/.

This is the blog of Stephanie Japel, a talented textile designer who has knit several patterns for *Knitty*, the online magazine. Japel is a glamorous,

New Mexican redhead with a fun sense of style. Like many knitting bloggers, she shares patterns, knitting tips, and photos of her knitting projects. One sweater she designed, called "Orangina," is quite sexy and stirred up a blogging buzz for a while.

Interweave Press, http://www.interweave.com/knit/projects_articles.asp.

This is the online accompaniment to books and magazines that Interweave Press publishes on fiber crafts, beading, and natural living. *Interweave Knits* is a popular read among contemporary knitters. This site offers free patterns, articles, product reviews, access to back issues, and subscription sales.

KnitKnit, http://www.knitknit.net/.

Enter here to discover the cutting edge of knitting. *KnitKnit* is a paper magazine devoted to contemporary fiber arts. It is the brainchild of artist and curator Sabrina Gschwandtner, who was interviewed for this book. Limited edition copies of *KnitKnit* have handmade covers created by a fine artist. You can read articles from sold-out issues of *KnitKnit* on the Web site, and you can also learn where to purchase available issues. More details on Gschwandtner and *KnitKnit* can be found in Chapter 5.

Knit Picks, http://www.knitpicks.com/.

Husband and wife team Bob and Kelley Petkun founded Knit Picks in 2002 to bring top quality yarns to knitters at low prices. Indeed, the prices for luxury fibers are better than fair, and many seasoned knitters swear by this outlet. Knitter's Review offers more detailed insights on Knit Picks' value, weighing quality, and price considerations.

Knit Swap, http://community.livejournal.com/knitswap/

Go here to trade unwanted yarn, books, or tools with other knitters. One girl's stash is another girl's treasure.

Knitta Please!, www.myspace.com/knittaplease.

A posse of young mothers and friends in the bohemian Houston, Texas neighborhood of Montrose plasters public spaces with bits of brightly colored, knitted graffiti. Trees, door handles, car antennae, lamp posts, bicycle racks—all are targets for Knitta, which tweaks the name of an explicit hip hop tune by Ol' Dirty Bastard. While commentators have noted that knitted grafitti subverts people's notions about both knitters and grafitti artists, the Knitta gang's motives appear to be more playful—they just want to cheer people up. They even include buttons that allow easy removal of their knitted tags. The Web site includes a gallery with photos of Knitta tag sightings from around the nation and the world, including a bit of knitted grafitti wrapping a stone on the Great Wall of China.

Knitter's Review, http://www.knittersreview.com/.

This site is a free, weekly online magazine for knitters that provides great reviews of knitting yarns, books, and tools. With all the alluring ways to fritter away your money on knitting supplies, it's good to check in here for a dose of objectivity.

The Knitting Fiend, http://www.thedietdiary.com/blog/.

A site for knitters ready to try designing their own patterns, but scared of the math involved. Lucia Liljegren offers a smorgasbord of knitting aids, including many calculators that do the math for spacing button holes, adding bust darts, figuring out how many balls of yarn you need for a project, increasing and decreasing evenly across a row, and much more.

Knitting Rock-Along, http://brainylady.blogspot.com/rock-along.htm.

Knitters want to rock! If you want to try intarsia (two-color knitting) but prefer skulls and flames to tulips and snowflakes, this is your site. The blogger named Brainy Lady hosts this gallery of rock 'n' roll knitting designs, including patterns that incorporate the international rock-on (IRO) symbol. That's the devil horn hand sign: lifted pointer and pinky fingers. Knit something rockin' and submit its photo to be posted on the site. Skulls, lightning bolts, and anarchy symbols, for those "not down with devil horns," as your hostess puts it.

Knitty, http://www.knitty.com/.

Knitty is the premier online knitting magazine. The free patterns published here are submitted by professionals and amateurs alike, and most are attractive, clear, and accurate. Editor Amy Singer imbues the publication with an upbeat, humorous, and modern tone. Layout and design are thoroughly modern and appealing. Somehow, *Knitty* successfully straddles the line between classic and contemporary. I have shared this web address with my mother, and she, too approves. For more about *Knitty*, see Chapter 8.

Lorna's Laces, http://www.lornaslaces.net/.

This yarn designer creates delicious hand-dyed yarns in beautiful colorways. Lion and Lamb, a 50/50 blend of wool and silk, is the yarn of choice for knitting the cult classic scarf, Clapotis. For more on Clapotis, see Chapter 8.

Mason-Dixon Knitting, http://www.masondixonknitting.com/.

The shared blog of two knitters whose friendship spans the Mason-Dixon Line: Kay Gardiner lives in New York, while Ann Shayne lives in Nashville, Tennessee. For years they never met other than virtually, but that has changed since the publication of their book, *Mason-Dixon Knitting: The Curious Knitter's Guide*. The book is full of cute patterns in inspired color combinations. The blog is funny, warm, and well written.

microRevolt, http://www.microrevolt.org/knitPro.htm.

Here, knitting is definitely a political act. The site microRevolt critiques worker exploitation, with projects about the history of sweatshop labor and scrutiny of mass production of garments, including the increasing globalization and feminization of the industry's workforce. One highlight of this

Web site is knitPro, a free knitting program that converts any graphic image into a knitting chart. Site creator Cat Mazza includes it because it lets one hijack familiar brand trademarks, but the program is useful to any two-color knitter, regardless of politics. Read on after you've exploited microRevolt's generosity in sharing knitPro. The site might make you feel better about overspending on yarn.

MK Carroll, http://mkcarroll.typepad.com/.

Few knitters and crocheters are as playful as MK Carroll, who makes funky retro toys and knick-knacks that are also more than a little weird. Carroll's pattern for a knitted womb (see "Strange Things People Knit," below) was featured in the online magazine *Knitty*, while her crocheted and knitted sushi roll/toilet paper roll cozy was published by Crochetme.com. Carroll is also known for knitting up sweet little outfits for Blythe dolls, whose big heads and wide, color-changing eyes were so scary to kids in the seventies that they were taken off the market.

The Prayer Shawl Ministry, http://www.shawlministry.com/.

Janet Bristow and Victoria Galo founded this ministry in 1998 to give knitters a way to offer both spiritual and physical comfort to people undergoing trial or change in their lives, whether it is grief, disease, hardship, growth, or celebration. The site offers patterns for shawls and a list of possible recipients, as well as inspiring stories shared by people who have given and received the shawls. Bristow and Galo encourage knitters to pray for the recipient throughout the process of making a shawl. A friend of mine in Sellersville, Pennsylvania, recounted how her neighbor, who is battling cancer, responded when she got a shawl from a local church's knitting ministry. The woman donned the shawl and felt, "wrapped in the comfort of friends I have yet to meet," she told my friend.

The Revolutionary Knitting Circle, http://knitting.activist.ca/.

A Canadian-based network of knitters with a manifesto that supports DIY values of helping people produce the goods they need to live without relying on corporations. The Web site offers patterns for peace-promoting banners, flags, and armbands. Visitors to the site are also encouraged to promote local DIY efforts by starting their own knitting circles. In June 2002, the Calgary faction of this loosely knit clan of activists joined other protesters at the G-8 summit in Kananaskis. The club carried their yarn and needles and knitted banners, and they cloaked trees in knitted cozies to symbolize protection against security forces that patrolled during the event. ("Group raises needles and yarn against globalization," *CBC News*, May 20, 2002.)

Rowan International, http://www.knitrowan.com/html/knitting_circle.asp.

This site offers a knitting club and magazine subscription in one. This is where one goes to join what is now considered one of the founding institutions of the online knitting world, the Rowanettes. Many a knitting blogger started out simply exchanging messages with other knitters using an electronic bulletin board like the one that Rowan provides for its paying members. Kay Gardiner recalled how when she first signed up for Rowan International, she started to worry that her knitting obsession might be getting "a little icky." But she went with it, and fewer than five years later, she found her life transformed by the knitting subculture.

Schoolhouse Press, http://www.schoolhousepress.com/about.htm.

Knitting innovator Elizabeth Zimmermann may no longer be with us, but her spirit lives on at Schoolhouse Press. Zimmermann founded the company in 1959 to supply knitters with pure wool and circular needles, which were both harder to find back then. In 1981, Zimmermann's daughter Meg Swansen began publishing books and instructional videos through the company. Today the Web site is where knitters anywhere can order DVDs of Zimmermann's classic Public Broadcasting System (PBS) program, "Knitting Workshop," which can be difficult to find elsewhere. Also, learn more about Knitting Camp, a tradition begun by Zimmermann and perpetuated by Swansen, where knitters get together for master lessons and knitters' reunions. A classic.

Steal This Sweater, http://www.stealthissweater.com/.

This is the Web site of fiber artist Lisa Anne Auerbach, who designs machine-knit sweaters with clever and often politically charged messages knitted into them. Auerbach is one of a few knitters who use knitting to make radical statements. "Stop making scarves. Start making trouble," she urges visitors to her site. Here you can download the free pattern for her brilliant Body Count Mittens, into which the maker knits the number of U.S. soldiers, or, if preferred, Iraqi civilians, killed in the war in Iraq. For a fuller explanation of Auerbach's inventive art, see Chapter 5.

Tess Designer Yarns, http://home.gwi.net/~tessyarn/.

This Maine-based provider of richly hand-dyed yarns in many luxury fibers appears pricey until you look at the size of the skeins. You can only really buy a lot of Tess yarns. If you must touch your yarn before you buy it, find the Tess booth at one of the fiber or knitting shows and conferences they frequent. The yarns look even better in person.

White Lies Designs, http://www.whiteliesdesigns.com/index.html.

Joan McGowan-Michael creates lacy, romantic knit designs for a wide range of sizes. Most notable are her lingerie items. Babydolls, camisoles, thongs, corsetlettes, and stockings are among the goodies to be found here. Back in the day, some of these patterns were free, but the designer must have realized she's got something special going. Patterns and kits are for sale.

Yarn-A-Go-Go, http://www.yarnagogo.com/.

Rachael Herron's blog is lots of fun to read, and it is also home to a spectacular gallery of tattoos inspired by an obsession with knitting. The gallery welcomes all knitters with tattoos to submit pictures of their body art, but what's remarkable is how many of these people have permanently marked them-selves with a symbol of their loyalty to the craft. "Born to Knit!" is scrawled under a tattoo on one man's chest that depicts a skull with crossed knitting needles slid through the eye sockets. "Knit Happens," proclaims another tat-too of a flaming ball of yarn. I'm betting these people view the knitting revo-lution as more than a fad. Read more about Herron in Chapter 8.

Yarn Boy, http://www.yarnboy.com/.

Yarn Boy is the blog and Web site of Jesse Loesberg, a San Franciscan who valiantly defends the honor and virility of male knitters everywhere. He has some information here on the history of male knitters, as well as an amusing knitting advice column, Ask Yarn Boy. Loesberg is also a professional writer, and he publishes some of his written work on the site. To learn more about Yarn Boy, see Chapter 5.

Yarn Harlot, http://www.yarnharlot.ca/blog/.

Diva of all knitting bloggers, Stephanie Pearl-McPhee publishes this highly humorous blog. She dubbed herself "Yarn Harlot" in an *Interweave Knits* article where she claimed she is so obsessed with yarn, she cannot be loyal to just one. See Chapter 8.

You Knit What?, http://youknitwhat.blogspot.com/.

This is the place to view what contributors to the site deem as the ugliest, weirdest, most amusing, or least practical knitted items. Creators, punk rock knitter and knitty kitty, no longer post to the site, but the archives are a satis-fying journey for the self-assigned design critic.

STRANGE THINGS PEOPLE KNIT

Brains: The Museum of Scientifically Accurate Brain Art, http://harbaugh.uoregon.edu/Brain/index.htm.

Click here for the world's largest collection of fabric brain art, all inspired by dissection and neuroscience. Karen Norberg's knitted version of a human brain is remarkable; the detail will leave some viewers squeamish and others enthralled.

Massive Rabbit, http://www.gelitin.net/mambo/index.php?set_albumName=album14&option=com_gallery_proj144&Itemid=91&include=view_album.php.

A group of four artists called Gelitin, based in Austria, positioned a giant, knitted bunny on a mountaintop in Italy in September 2005. This Web site affords you several bird's eye views of the huge, floppy creature atop Colletto Fava in the village of Artesina in Italy's Piedmont region. The site also offers a somewhat cryptic explanation of the project, which was slated to remain in place for twenty years.

Wedding, http://castoff.info/album.asp.

> Cast Off, the UK-based knitting club for boys and girls, which organizes knitting circles in public places, planned a wedding for which everything, except the participants, was knitted. Keeping with nuptial traditions, they also compiled a photo album for your pleasure. See knitted doves, knitted cake, knitted tea sandwiches, knitted candles, knitted champagne bottles, and, of course, a knitted dress.

> Cast Off also sells an array of goofy knitted items, including a cigarette, lipstick, penis (with cables posing as veins), grenade, and big toe protector. Seeing is believing.

Womb, http://www.knitty.com/ISSUEwinter04/PATTwomb.html.

> Knitter and crocheter MK Carroll of Honolulu, Hawaii, designed this adorable uterus doll for *Knitty*. Though she was taking anatomy and physiology courses at the time that she contrived this gem, she concedes it's not entirely accurate in terms of scale, color, or details. Who cares? It's the cutest womb ever.

> For something even funnier, check out this photo of the womb knitting: http://www.knitty.com/blog/archives/2005_01_01_knittyblogarchive.html.

BLOGS

One more thing about knitting Web sites: there are so many out there that I have not studied with any regularity, including at least a thousand blogs. You may find, as I have, that exploring blogs is a good way to eat up a day. Rather than recommend to you the blogs that captured my interest, based on my taste, I will simply list a bunch whose names struck my fancy. I do this because knitting seems to lend itself to puns and clever wordplay, and knitting bloggers exploit this fact to its full effect.

Crazy Aunt Purl
Dirty Purls
Enchanting Juno
Femiknitz
Fluffa!
Knit and Tonic
Knitgrrl
Knitters Anonymous
The Knitting Curmudgeon
Moth Heaven
The Needle and the Damage Done
Stitchy McYarnPants
Super Eggplant

INDEX

ABOUT THE AUTHOR

KERRY WILLS, an avid knitter herself, is a journalist and former corporate communications specialist.